Lou'

s. Norton

MW01064106

CHAINS BROKEN

With seeds of faith sown and watered by the Holy Spirit

Written by Sherry Norton

WESTBOW
PRESS
A DIVISION OF THOMAS NELSON

WestBow Press books may be ordered through booksellers or by contacting:

WestBow Press
A Division of Thomas Nelson
1663 Liberty Drive
Bloomington, IN 47403
www.westbowpress.com
1-(866) 928-1240

ISBN: 978-1-4497-2489-4 (sc)
ISBN: 978-1-4497-2488-7 (ebk)

Library of Congress Control Number: 2011914943

Printed in the United States of America

WestBow Press rev. date: 09/23/2011

Contents

01. NOTHING WITHOUT YOU

Written August 1998

I am nothing without you,
a piece of dirt from which I grew,
Loving hands have molded me,
like a potter with his clay.

Sons of God, Joint Heiress with Christ,
Kings and Priests, who have won the fight,
God's mighty army, whose battle is won,
with Jesus at its head.

When the sun shall cease to shine,
and the moon turns to blood,
Jesus comes back in the clouds,
and takes us all away.

We are nothing without you,
A piece of dirt from which we grew,
Loving hands have molded us,
like a potter with his clay. Amen.

02. THE OPEN DOOR

Written May 1999

When the Jews rejected Him,
the door was open for me,
And when they led Him up the hill,
they nailed Him to a tree.
All the blood He shed;
He shed for you and me,
all the blood He shed;
He shed for you and me.

They laid Him in a borrowed tomb,
it looked like death had won,
But early on the third day,
behold Gods Son.
Jesus rose up from the grave;
life flowed through Him,
Jesus rose up from the grave;
life flowed through Him.

Jesus Christ the Lamb of God,
who shed His blood for thee,
won the battle over death,
and came forth victoriously.
Who stands before His Father God;
for you and me!
Who stands before His Father God;
for you and me!

When His word has been fulfilled,
before this earth is done,
we go to meet our Saviour,
and become one.
God's mighty army has come,
God's mighty army has come. Amen.

03. BLESSED

Written May 1999

Blessed is the Lord,
and blessed is His name,
and blessed are His people.

He shall feed His sheep,
and lead us all to drink,
and Deliver us from evil.

Light is all around,
hope doth abound,
and joy fills His people.

Blessed is the Lord,
and blessed is His name,
and blessed are His people. Amen.

04. COME, LEARN, SING AND REJOICE

Written May 1999

Come unto me O child come,
with Love—Trust and Faith.
Learn of me O child learn,
of Gods mercy and grace.
Sing with me O child sing,
I arose up from the grave.
Rejoice in me O child rejoice,
My Love fills this place. Amen.

05. DEFEATED HE WAS NOT

Written May 1999

To be like Jesus is all I ask,
The Prince of peace is He,
The fairest of ten thousands was nailed upon a tree.

They laid His body in a tomb,
and sealed it with a rock,
My Lord of lords and King of kings defeated He was not.

Rejoice and praise His Holy Name,
and dry your sad-sad eyes,
Our Redeemer liveth and gained the prize.

Jesus is the Lamb of God,
who shed His blood for thee,
He took us out of darkness into victory.

He opened eyes-ears and hearts,
and made us whole again.
Blessed is the Son of God,
who freed us from sin. Amen.

06. SEE

Written May 1999

See the Lily of the valley,
see the sparrow fall,
see the lovely rose of Sharon,
And see how spring doth call.

See the mountain up so high,
see the mighty oak,
see the river flowing by,
And see the fog and smoke.

See the stars up in the sky,
see the waterfall,
see the sands upon the beach,
And see He loves us all.

See the rain falling down,
see the garden grow,
see the flowers of the field,
and see the lava flow.
see our Saviour on a tree,
see He shed His blood for thee,
see He died and rose again,
And see now we are free from sin. Amen.

07. MY CHOSEN PATH

Written May 1999

I walked down the path till it became two,
I chose the narrow path,
for it drew few.
Step by step I go on this narrow path;
step by step I go looking not back.

This path isn't easy,
but neither is it hard,
my Lord and Saviour carried me when I got tired.
Day by day I go with Jesus at my side;
day by day I go his word is my guide.

Sometimes I rest along the way,
sometimes I run the race,
and sometimes I look into a glass and darkly see His face.
Foot by foot the day is done;
foot-by-foot, the race is run.

The light it shines upon my path,
darkness then is driven back,
He bids me eat and drink my fill and know that Jesus Christ is real.
Piece by piece I am sealed;
piece-by-piece He is revealed.

He makes me King and Priest on High,
Chosen Son of God am I,
pressing on towards the mark to my crown, my robe and music like a
harp.
Line by line His love is shown;
line by line Gods Son is known. Amen.

08. CHAINS BROKEN

Written May 1999

I thought I knew my Lord and God;
but darkness filled my mind.
I thought I knew my Saviour's word;
most all I knew was lies.
Fear-ignorance-bondage and control,
was mostly all my mind did know.

One day my life began to change,
My Lord and God did rearrange.
The chains did break and I was free,
my Lord and God He spoke to me.

my soul was starved and very dry;
His presents was for what it cried.
I love to praise His Holy Name;
Gods love has been my glorious gain.

When there are people who lead us astray;
we have to learn to forgive them and pray.
That their souls I will forgive;
and Gods love in them shall live. Amen.

09. FACE WHAT YOU DON'T LIKE

Written May 1999

Strolling down the road of life,
not knowing what was in store,
I tried to build myself a wall,
not wanting to see anymore.

I tried to hide myself away;
I tried to keep the wolf at bay.
After many years I awoke;
knowing that my wall was broke.
Life has been marching by;
wait for me I wanted to cry.

All I know is I have to face,
that I am in the human race.
Building walls and closing eyes,
won't keep time from passing by. Amen

10. THE HOME I BUILT IN MY MIND

Written—May 1999

The house I built in my mind;
was made with bricks-oak and pine.
With cedar shakes on it's crown;
and lots of windows all around.

The walls and floors are sealed up tight;
no cracks for water-wind or light.
The windows are snug in their frames;
the doors are hung just the same.

The chimney bricks were laid with care;
the bedrooms they are all upstairs.
The lights are bright in every room;
that way they don't look like a tomb.

I like my kitchen full of sun;
I don't think I'm the only one.
The porches they are all closed in;
this pleases me not my men.

The sheds where they'll find pleasure so;
the tools they'll use to rake and mow.
To shovel away the falling snow;
to sit and watch the garden grow.

The flowering bushes around our place;
bring a joyous smile to our face.
The trees that shade us from the sun;
bring us pleasure every one.

With lots of cabinets and shelves inside;
this is the home I have built in my mind. Amen

11. I THANK YOU

Written June 1999

I thank You for your Love,
I thank You for my life,
and I thank you for your mercies and walking by my side.

I thank You for your grace,
I thank You for my health,
and I thank You for your Peace that passes all understanding.

I thank You for your wisdom,
I thank You for my talents,
and I thank You for your Son, whom has set me free.

I thank You for your Strength,
I thank You for my armor,
and I thank You for your truth that your Spirit shows to me.

I thank You for your patience,
I thank You for my gift,
and I thank You for your word, which guides my path to you.

I thank you for your covenants,
I thank You for my promises,
and I thank You for Your light, which shines throughout the world.

I can never thank You enough for all you have done for me,
but as long as there is breath and life,
I will thank you through eternity. Amen

12. WHO AND WHERE IS

Written July 1999

Who is God? Don't you know? He is our creator.
Who is Jesus? Don't you know? He is our Lord and Saviour.
Who is the Holy Ghost? Don't you know? He is our comforter and
friend.
Where is God? Don't you know? In the third heaven.
Where is Jesus? Don't you know? Seated on the right hand of His Father.
Where is The Holy Ghost? Don't you know? He is everywhere.

If ye are seeking; then ye shall find answers to these questions.
If ye knock; the door shall open to guidance and direction.
When we except Jesus Christ as Saviour of our soul,
our Lord and God Almighty brings us into the fold.
In knowing the Father, you must know the Son,
and finally find His abiding Love.
There is no price that we must pay,
god has already made the way. Amen

13. JESUS CHRIST IS

Written July 1999

Jesus Christ is the Light of the World,
focus on Him;
Jesus Christ is the Light of the World,
He shall free us from sin.

Jesus Christ is the Lamb of God,
who shed His blood for thee;
Jesus Christ is the Lamb of God,
who set His people free.

Jesus Christ is the Son of God,
who sits on the right hand of His Father;
Jesus Christ is the Son of God,
who the wine, was turned from water.

Jesus Christ is our Lord and Saviour,
who sacrificed Himself for us;
Jesus Christ is our Lord and Saviour,
who bought us with His blood.

Jesus Christ is our Redeemer,
who died and lives again;
Jesus Christ is our Redeemer,
who freed us from sin. Amen

14. CHOICES

Written September 1999

There are choices in our lives,
every day we live,
make these choices for the right,
and see what God shall give.

Light instead of darkness on this path we walk.
Love instead of hatred for our fellow man.
Wisdom instead of foolishness to build our house on the rock.
Knowledge instead of ignorance for all God's plan for man.

There are choices in our lives,
every day we live,
make these choices for the right,
and see what god shall give;
As for me,
I choose the Lord. Amen

15. THE ROAD

Written September 1999

This road I am on it leads to two,
which one will you follow?
The one called truth or the other lies,
which one can you swallow?

This road I am on it leads to two,
which one can you see?
The one called light or the other dark,
which will set you free?

This road I am on it leads to two,
which one can you walk?
The one called narrow or the other wide,
which one leads to the rock? Amen

16. ONE HEARTS CRY

Written September 1999

Change me Lord, this I pray, mold me like a piece of clay.
Teach me Lord, this I ask, polish me like brass.
Use me Lord, this I plea that all the glory be to thee. Amen.

17. GOD IS GREATER THAN ALL

Written October 1999

God is greater than all,
and we should put our trust in him.
Man is weak and tends to fall,
and without Him we can do nothing of ourselves.

God is greater than all,
and we should totally rely on Him.
Man sometimes fails to see others needs,
but God sees all,
and is mindful of those who come to Him and believe.

God is greater than all,
and we should totally lean on Him.
Man can't,
by leaning on his own understanding-he faints,
but for those who lean on God, He will never leave nor forsake.
God is our strength. Amen

18. JESUS IS

Written November 1999

Jesus is Love,
love is the key that opens our heart.
Jesus is Light,
the Light is a lamp unto our feet.
Jesus is the Prince of Peace,
the Peace that passes all understanding.
Jesus is the Lord of lords,
the Lord and Saviour of our soul.
Jesus is the King of kings,
the King who sits upon His throne.
Jesus is the Lamb of God,
the Lamb who shed His blood for thee.
Jesus is god Son and Christ,
the Christ who won the battle over death and came forth victoriously.
Amen.

19. LIKE THE

Written November 1999

Like the sewer of the seed,
God's seed was sown in me.
Like the tree baring fruit,
God's fruit was born in me.
Like the water quenching thirst,
Gods living water abides within.
Like the flour making bread,
Gods Son's own body is the bread of life for men.
Like the Sun that gives us light,
Gods own Son gives light of life.
Like the man who marries his wife,
the bridegroom waits to wed His bride. Amen.

20. THE BEST CHOICE

Written November 1999

Able gave of his first fruits,
it was a lamb, he gave,
but Jesus Christ, the Lamb of God,
gave of Him self one day.

Abraham believing God,
offered up his son,
but Jesus Christ, Gods only begotten Son,
became the victorious one.

David loved God,
a man after His own heart,
but Jesus loves all,
the whole not the part. Amen

21. THE BOOK

Written November 1999

There is a book I like to read,
whose words dwell in my heart.
There is a book I like to read,
whose words set me apart.

There is a book that tells me of,
a pure and simple love.
There is a book that tells me of,
a heaven up above.

There is a book that shows me,
who has made this earth.
There is a book that shows me,
how much more I am worth.

There is a book that leads me from,
darkness into light.
There is a book that leads me from,
death into life.

There is a book that keeps me on,
this narrow way.
There is a book that keeps me from,
sinning day by day.

This book that I have spoken of,
I hope you find it too.
God's peace and love for all mankind,
His Son has already proved. Amen

22. A PLEA OF A HOPEFUL HEART

Written November 1999

By His stripes,
Ye are healed.
By His Word,
He is revealed.
Jesus died,
to set man free.
Jesus' blood,
was shed for thee.

To keep His light,
upon My way.
To be as gold,
instead of hay.
To be filled with love,
instead of fear. To be joined with Him, who dried my tears.

Jesus is the Light,
of the world.
Jesus' love,
is more precious than pearls. Amen

23. SONGS OF WORSHIP

Written January 2000

I shall bless the Lord at all times,
His praise shall continually be in my mouth.
Let the temples be filled with His glory,
and the courts be filled with His praise,
I shall trust in Jesus to show me the way.
How great is our God,
how great is His name He is the greatest one,
for ever the same,
For holy is the Lord and mighty is His name,
King of Heaven but down to earth He came.
For here is my rest forever and here will I dwell,
with my Lord and Saviour,
learning to be like Him.
Just as I am Lord,
without one plea,
but that thy blood was shed for thee,
for He is able,
yes more than able to carry me through. Amen.

24. LIFTING UP THE NAME OF JESUS

Written January 2000

Everybody ought to know who Jesus is,
who made the mountains and who made the trees,
and who made the rivers that flowed to the sea.

So let's talk about Jesus,
and what He means to me.

Jesus is He who,
healed the broken hearted and made the blind to see,
He made the lame to walk again and He set the captives free,
He loves the little children and loves you and me.

Jesus is the rock on which I stand,
and the air in which I breathe,
the joy in my heart and the song that I sing,
He is the Shepherd of the sheep and He takes good care of me.

Jesus is the Rose of Sharon,
the Lilly of the Valley is He,
the King of kings and Lord of lords,
Mighty God indeed,
Jesus is the Lamb of God who shed His blood for thee. Amen

25. CREATURES GREAT AND SMALL REJOICE

Written—January 2000

There are trees outside my window,
where birds make their nests,
and everyday about daybreak,
they awake from their rest.
And greet the morning with a song,
music fills the air.
And greet the morning with a song,
heir long their music they share.
God's love is like the sunrise,
rolling back the dark.
God's love is like the campfire,
whose warmth fills our hearts.

When winter is finished blasting its freeze,
upon this earth we live,
spring comes forth refreshed and new,
and flowers begin to bloom.
All creatures' great and small,
brighten like a new moon.
All creatures great and small,
begin to sing a new tune.
God's love is like a fortress,
into which I can run.
God's love is like glue,
where two are joined as one.

From jungle to prairie, and ocean to lake,
mountain to valley,
God's creations are great.
From smallest to small and biggest to big,
God's creations are marvelous as long as they live.

From smallest to small and biggest to big,
God's creations are marvelous He made them for men.
God's love is like a sunset,
beautiful in all its glory.
God's love is like a baby's smile,
it tells the whole story. Amen

26. A MAN'S QUESTION ANSWERED

Written January 2000

There was a man who stopped and asked this question of me.
How do you know there is a God and where is He?
All I could do was look at him,
and then my answer came from within.

Do you see those trees?
Do you hear those birds?
Do you feel that breeze upon your skin?

Have you seen the mountains capped with snow?
Have you seen the valleys down below?
Have you seen the flowers grow?

Did you see that bird on the wing?
Did you see the stars gleam?
Did you see the flowing stream?

How about that rainbow after the rain?
How about that bear in the cane?
How about nothing being the same?

Yes: there is a living God,
and He is everywhere we look,
open your heart and receive His love,
and ye shall not be forsook. Amen

27. MAGNIFICENT CREATURES OF GOD

Written—February 2000

The horse is important to our history,
on this earth we live.

A magnificent creature created by God,
for man He did give.

He stands for power-strength and speed,
The mustang stood for being wild and free.

Till man began to capture his spirit,
the saddle-bridle and the bit weren't near it.

In order for man to control his way,
the bridle and bit were put in their place.

Like God who holds the reins in His hands,
through His word He leads and we must follow.

He teaches us the things we should know,
He teaches us the way we should go.

Unlike the horse for often is no care,
God does not give us more than we are able to bear.

Jesus came as man to set all free,
I love the horse but I'm glad I am me. Amen

28. HANDS

Written February 2000

Hands holding hands strengthening the bonds.
Hands healing anointed by God.

Hands helping man pulling us out of the fire.
Hands reaching down pulling us up out of the mire.
Hands gentle and soft for all those God has called and loves.
Hands hard in judgment for all those whom have chosen nothing from
above.
Jesus' hands are stretched out wide,
He bids us come and be renewed in Life. Amen

29. PURCHASED BY HIS BLOOD

Written February 2000

Buy gold that thou mayest be rich.
Buy oil that thou mayest see.
Buy food that thou mayest be filled.
By the shedding of His blood,
He cleansed me.
By thy fruit,
ye shall know them.
By thy truth,
ye shall be set free.
By thy word,
thy bond is given.
By thy blood,
He purchased me.
Buy silver,
refined by the fire.
Buy cattle,
for its meat.
Buy sheep,
for its wool.
By the water,
God's love flows in me. Amen

30. JESUS SWEET JESUS

Written—February 2000

Jesus sweet Jesus,
God's only begotten son.
Jesus sweet Jesus,
the fairest of ten thousands.

Jesus sweet Jesus,
the prince of peace is He.
Jesus sweet Jesus,
who set the captives free.

Jesus sweet Jesus,
who died and lives again.
Jesus sweet Jesus,
who freed us from sin. Amen

31. GOD THE SUN

Written February 2000

With eyes like flames of fire,
a sword coming out of His mouth,
a golden girdle around His paps,
and feet as fine brass.
A countenance brighter than the sun,
with hair as white wool,
riding a white horse,
ruling with a rod of iron.
He is the same today-yesterday and forever,
the Alpha and omega-the First and the Last and the beginning and the
End.
He is the Lord of the harvest,
the Head of the Church,
the Great I Am,
and the Bridegroom waiting for His bride.
He walks among the seven lamp stands,
and holds the seven stars in His hand,
which broke the seven seals,
and judges' man.
Who bares us about in His body,
and holds us in His hands,
who sits on the right hand of His Father,
and waits for the finished plan.
With a voice that sounds like thunder,
and a whisper on the wind,
or many-many waters,
or a trumpet blast.
A roaring lion,
or a meek lamb,
a gentle dove,
or True God and True man. Amen

32. DO YOU KNOW WHERE LOVE IS?

Written Feb, 2000

Do you know where love is?
I have felt love from my Grandmother,
But, where is love?
I have felt love from my brother,
But, where is love?
I have felt love from my friends,
But, where is love?
The truest love I have ever had,
came from the truest man ever known,
He gave His life for all mankind,
and died that we can live,
Jesus; in Him,
There, is love! Amen.

33. A WANDERER WANDERING

Written—February 2000

A wanderer wandering through a land,
a stranger in this place.
A wanderer wandering through this land,
not knowing,
what there was to face.

From wilderness to valley,
from desert to mountain top high,
from miry road to rocky road,
from wet road to dry.

A wanderer wandering in a land,
with Jesus as my guide.
A wanderer wandering in this land,
His love keeps me alive. Amen

34. HELP WANTED!

Written February 2000

Help wanted,
not advertised,
silent crying heart.
Help wanted,
crying heart,
for open listening ears.
Help wanted,
so many questions,
please don't mind the tears.
Help wanted,
silent cries,
don't really know where to start.
Help wanted,
silent plea,
I need some ones open heart.
Help wanted,
not advertised,
hugs and words are apart. Amen.

35. THE AUTHOR

Written March 2000

If God is for us,
who can be against us?
No weapon formed against us can prosper.
If God is for us,
who can be against us?
No name is above the name of the Author.
If God is for us,
who can be against us?
No calamity comes nigh our dwelling.
If God is for us,
who can be against us?
Come finisher of our faith there is no prevailing.
If God is for us,
who can be against us?
His blood cleansed us from sin.
If God is for us,
who can be against us?
The door was opened He welcomes us in.
If God is for us,
who can be against us?
If I be lifted up I will draw all men unto me.
If God is for us,
who can be against us?
He set the captives free in victory. Amen.

36. BEAUTY PRACTICALLY DESTROYED

Written March 2000

I contemplate O so many things,
that God has created for our enjoyment.
Whether in a meadow-or the woods,
or a mountaintop high,
or a valley-or a plateau,
or the desert nearby,
or a canyon-or a cave,
or a seaside shore.
There are colors and shapes,
and vistas breath takenly beautiful.
There are plants-and animals,
and birds for us to enjoy.
There are stars that glitter,
like diamonds on velvet.
There are sunrises and sunsets,
which simple words cannot describe it.
I contemplate O so many things,
that God has done for man,
but question not these things of beauty,
that God has so graciously planned.
God given beauty that was created for our enjoyment,
but why has man practically destroyed it? Amen.

37. NOT FOR LONG HIS BED

Written March 2000

The foxes have holes and the birds have nests,
but the Son of man hath no place to lay His head.
The fish have their schools,
and the ball players have their teams,
and the Lamb of God was sacrificed alone for thee.
The rain has its rainbow,
and the door its key,
and the Shepherd of the sheep was who died to set man free.
The rose has thorns,
and the oceans its seas,
while Jesus was who was nailed on a tree.
The fire has its flame,
and the lettuce its head,
and Christ's tomb not for long was His bed. Amen.

38. LORD YOU DIDN'T HAVE TO DO IT!

Written March 2000

At of the deep void of dark,
You spoke the light,
and spoke this world into existence.
Lord you did not have to do it,
but I am glad that you did!

From the dust and the dirt,
and your holy breath,
you fashioned man in your own image.
Lord you did not have to do it,
but I am glad that you did!

Even when man fell in sin,
and became your enemy,
you bore with him and made another way.
Lord you did not have to do it,
but I am glad that you did!

You loved us so much that You gave,
You're only begotten Son.
Lord You did not have to do it,
but I am glad that you did!

And Jesus loved us so much,
that He was willing to hang on the cross shedding His blood,
to die and rise again in victory.
Lord You didn't have to do it,
but I am glad,
oh' so very glad that You did! Amen.

39. SUFFICIENT GRACE

Written March 2000

Out of the darkness came the light,
in the beginning was the word.
There is no loss in abundance,
in Christ Jesus all our needs are met.

Out of despair,
gave ye hope.
Unto us a child is born,
unto us a son is given.

Putting down hatred,
and showing forth love.
For which, God said,
"My grace is sufficient".

Deny foolishness,
and obtain wisdom.
For thine is the wisdom,
and the power and the glory forever.

Wipe out ignorance,
with a flood of knowledge.
Show me thy ways oh' Lord,
teach me thy ways to go.

Forsake war,
and embrace peace.
And if I be lifted up,
I will draw all men unto me. Amen.

40. LEARNING WAR NO MORE.

Written March 2000

They shall beat their swords into plow shears,
and their spears into pruning hooks.
Nations shall not lift sword up against nation,
neither shall they learn war anymore.
For our Lord of Lords and King of kings,
prince of peace indeed is setting up his kingdom,
for his thousand-year reign on this earth you see.

But everyone shall sit under his vine,
and his fig tree,
and no one shall make them afraid.
For the mouth of the Lord has spoken,
for all people each in the name of his god,
but we will walk in the name of the Lord our God,
forever and ever.
For the Lord of lords and King of kings,
Prince of peace indeed is setting up His kingdom,
for His thousand-year reign on this earth you see.
For the Lord of lords and King of kings,
Prince of Peace indeed is setting up His kingdom,
for His thousand-year reign on this earth you see. Amen.

41. HOPE STILL

Written April 2000

What ever your hand finds to do,
do it with all your might.
The race is not to the swift,
nor the battle to the strong.
Nor bread to the wise,
nor riches to men of understanding.
Nor favor to men of skill.
For time and chance happen to them all,
for man also does not know his time.
Like fish caught in a cruel net,
like birds caught in a snare.
Though the sons of men are snared,
in an evil time when it falls suddenly upon them.
So that which you must do, do quickly.
Ask and it shall be given,
seek and you shall find,
knock and the door shall be opened unto you.
I am the truth-the way and the life,
No man cometh unto the Father,
lest he come through me.
I am the door come,
enter in saith the Lord my God,
Come for he who asks shall be given,
he who seeks shall find,
he who knocks the door shall be open unto him. Amen.

42. FROM FIRST TO LAST

Written April 2000

In the beginning was nothing,
until it was spoken into existence.
Nothing that was created,
created He not for a particular purpose.
With a mathematical and artistic eye,
as to proportions and sizes,
and shapes and colors.
And a winsome and musical ear,
as to sound and melody,
and harmony and pitch of tone.
He orchestrates it all,
while in the third heaven sitting on His throne.
Though He never forces us,
or makes us do a thing,
we are not puppets on a marionette string.
Our will and our choices are our very own,
though He wills that no one is lost,
we have to choose and count the cost.
So please do not question,
why this or why that,
all we know is that God is master from beginning to end,
and first to last. Amen.

43. PAID IN FULL

Written April 2000

The loveliest rose that I have ever seen,
is a blood red rose that reminded me,
of the blood that was shed while He was nailed to the tree.

What's that you say Who was He,
that was nailed to the tree?
He was the Lamb of God who did no sin,
wrongfully accused and His Fathers only begotten son.

The lion of Judah who sits upon His throne,
Emanuel whose love He did show.

The Messiah whose battle was not with man,
but the prince of darkness of this land.

His only crime was His love for man,
and following His Father's plan.

For this they nailed Him to the tree.
Drop by drop His blood was shed,
washing away my sins.
All that kept us away from God,
was placed upon Him then.

Then they took Him off the tree,
when life had fled away.
They placed Him in a borrowed tomb,
until the third day.

That's when the rock was rolled away,
and God said,
"come forth my son".

Jesus won the battle over death,
He is the victorious one.
Yes, the debt has been paid in full,
for all those who come unto Him.
Yes, the debt has been paid in full,
when He said "IT IS FINISHED"! Amen.

44. CHRISTMAS

Written April 2000

Hustle and bustle and rushing about,
going hither and yon galore.
Tis the season for making merry,
though I wonder do we really know what for?
All the commercials on TV and the ad's run,
buy this and buy that,
and make things lots more fun.
But what is Christmas really all about?
It's not for filling the coffers.
It's about a Father who loved so much that He gave,
and His Son who became the door.
A baby who grew up and became a man,
was Lord and a lot more.
He was the blameless sacrificial lamb,
who shed His blood for thee.
Who said "Father forgive them for they know not what they do",
while nailed to the tree.
On the third day after being placed in the tomb,
His sealed stone was rolled away,
and Jesus came forth life flowing through Him in the glory of His
Father.
"I go and prepare a place for you that where I am ye may be also",
this is what Our Lord and Saviour said before He ascended on high in
the clouds.
And that's what Christmas should be all about,
the love and the gift God gave.
It's better to give than receive,
in Jesus name believe. Amen.

45. BIRTHS.

Written April 2000

Dreams and desires, desires and dreams,
they swirl about like vapor and mist,
seemingly elusive but grab hold and see.
We catch and try to hold but from afar,
we try to make it come to us but wrong we are.

To fulfill those desires and dreams that have been birthed,
we have to change to know their worth.
At times it seems that so much is in the way,
and others seemly zoom forth day by day.

His ways are not our ways and His thoughts are higher than our
thoughts,
but we need to be willing to be used as,
like certain tools of certain jobs.
Here am I My God,
He rules. Amen.

46. THE BURDEN TAKER

Written April 2000

Come unto me as a little child,
you who are heavy burdened,
and I will give you rest and peace,
joy and strength for the hurting.
What's that you say,
I have to much wrong my soul is black,
I am to far gone.
If Jesus were standing here,
He would say Oh' no,
my child these hands were stretched out wide for you,
give me a chance to show that my love is true.
Jesus took on Himself all that was evil and bad,
all our sins and all our iniquity,
and all our blemishes too.
Then we come to Him,
and except Him as our Lord and Saviour,
our Jesus Christ.
The shedding of His blood cleanses us from all sin,
never to be remembered against us anymore,
not by the father.

Then old things are passed away and all things have become new.
We are a new creature in Christ Jesus,
and united with our Father forever more.
Come unto me as a little child,
you who are lost and unwanted.
I leave the 99 and go after the 1 that is lost.
If I be lifted up I will draw all men unto me.
God so loved the world that He gave His only begotten Son,
that who so ever believeth on Him should not parish but have
everlasting life.
God said "I would that no one parish but that all would come unto me
and have a saving knowledge of Jesus Christ".
He wants to be our Father-our protector,
our Lord-our love,
for God is Love,
not just to the few but to all.
Come unto Him as a little child,
and let Him take your burdens,
He is so much stronger and wants to so very much,
but He will not force us it is our decision. Amen.

47. UNDER CONSTRUCTION

Written April 2000

Crash-boom watch out I plea,
Here is your hardhat and visor,
from the flying debris.

Do you see that sign,
hanging there?
What does it read?
In bold black letters it reads,
This site is under construction,
walk carefully.

This is how it is when my Father,
begins a new work in me,
I am under construction,
walking carefully.

No stumbling or tripping,
or being felled like a tree,
like a potter with his clay,
and a sculptor chipping away,
being consumed by His fire,
purified and lifted higher.

Trading in the hardhat and visor,
for my helmet-shield,
and sword of the spirit entire.

Under construction yes,
that is what I am,
finished and complete not yet,
but it's in the plan. Amen.

48. ONE'S COMMITMENT

Written April, 2000

What does it mean to commit,
to make a commitment?
Does it mean being there,
only when things are going well?
When we are benefited and blessed,
and things are going our way?
When we don't have to struggle,
even through hard places,
or suffer a little bit maybe?
When we don't have to put anything out of ourselves,
and are always looking to receive?
When our focus is on self being taken care of,
and are at our ease?
No, that to me would be a lonely-lonely world.
Without the love, grace,
and selfless act of our heavenly Father,
and Lord we would not be here.
Where all have sinned,
and fallen short of the glory of God.
Though He knew that He would have to descend from heaven,
away from His heavenly Father,
and be born as a man child on this earth.
Though He knew that He would have to suffer persecution,
verbal and physical abuse,
and rejection.

Though He was homeless-lied on,
Betrayed and put on trial,
though all He did was commit to doing His Fathers will,
and becoming hope,
of eternal life to all those who believe on Him.
He took all of our sins,
Iniquity and blemishes upon Himself. He was scourged-spit upon,
mocked and nailed to a tree,
and He died a guilty mans death,
who was not guilty for you and me.
But behold on the third day,
after being placed in a tomb,
He rose again victoriously.
So rejoice our promise is sure,
of everlasting life,
with our heavenly Father,
through His Son.
The results of Jesus'
commitment to love,
Honor and obey His Father.
Gaining the victory over sin,
Death-hell and the grave,
waiting for that day of His
second coming.
When He will come gather,
all those who have,
committed their lives unto Him,
and His Father. Amen.

49. DO YOU HEAR THE CRIES?

Written April 2000

Are you hearing their cries for help,
Listen you can hear their pain,
and despair.

The fields are ripe for harvest,
but the laborers are few,
how many more will die without me,
sayeth the Lord.

Come bring them as my sheep,
you are blessed who have come to me,
and have been adopted into the royal family.

But there are way too many who have not,
unless you come and do your part,
you'll keep hearing the cry of their heart.

Help me I'm falling,
there is no hope,
help me I am afraid,
is anyone there,
does anyone care?
Who will go,
who will say,
send me Lord-send me! Amen.

50. YEA NOT NAY

Written April 2000

Standing at the crossroads of this lonely road,
looking for a sign to know which way to go.

Lord I just don't know,
do I go or stay,
and which way help me I pray.

Sitting with the Holy Book,
searching for a glimmer of light,
decisions all around,
desiring to make them right.

Lord I love you,
but I just don't understand,
my heart cries Lord what do I do,
sit here,
even then I know that my hope is in you.

Child knowest that it is not by thy might,
nor thy power but my spirit,
sayeth the Lord.

Whether you are walking down a lonely road,
that seems to be darkened,
or seeking and searching for instruction,
and to be enlightened,
"I will never leave thee nor forsake thee",
sayeth the Lord.

if thou lookest unto me from which cometh thy strength,
follow me and let me take thy burdens,
and lighten thy path.

For my yoke is easy and thy burdens are light to me,
My word is a lamp unto thy feet,
and a light unto thy pathway,
sayeth the Lord thy God.
I am the truth,
the light and the way,
any man that cometh unto me,
I will in no wise turn away,
so come unto me and say yea not nay. Amen.

51. HOPE IN JESUS

Written April 2000

You have drawn me out of darkness,
into the marvelous light,
now standing at the throne in the presents of my God,
falling at His feet,
like dead but yet alive,
even in the darkness there is light,
now sitting with Jesus at our Fathers right.

There is hope in Jesus,
all along the way,
there is hope in Jesus,
who turned night into day,
there is hope in Jesus,
who shed His blood for me,
there is hope in Jesus,
who set the captive free.

Light the darkened pathway with God's Holy Word,
looking unto Jesus,
in death and rebirth,
the loving Shepherd God's sacrificial lamb,
who bore all on His shoulders,
is the Great I Am,
so look up to the hills,
from wince comes our help.

And put your hope in Jesus,
all along the way,
put your hope in Jesus,
who turned night into day,
put your hope in Jesus,
who shed His blood for thee,
put your hope in Jesus,
who set the captive free.

Look upon our Lord,
nailed upon the tree,
who said if I be lifted up,
I will draw all men unto me,
shedding His blood He died,
was buried and rose again for you and me,
to set all free who believe.

So my hope is in Jesus,
all along the way,
and my hope is in Jesus,
who turned night into day,
and my hope is in Jesus,
who shed His blood for me,
and my hope is in Jesus,
who set this captive free. Amen.

52. NUGGETS OF GOLD REVEALED

Written April 2000

The heavens declare the glory of God,
and the firmaments show His handy work,
day unto day utters speech,
and night unto night reveals knowledge,
their light has gone through out all the earth,
and the their words to the end of the world,
in them He has set a tabernacle for the sun,
which is like the bride groom coming out of his chamber,
and rejoiceth like a strong man,
to run his race.
The law of the Lord is perfect converting the soul,
the testimony of the Lord is sure making wise the simple,
the statutes of the Lord are right rejoicing the heart,
the commandment of the Lord is pure enlightening the eye,
the fear of the Lord is clean enduring for ever the judgments of the Lord
are true,
and righteous all together.
More are they to be desired,
are they than gold,
sweeter also than the honey in the honey comb,
oh' Lord,
thou art my strength,
and my redeemer,
blessed be the rock,
and let the God of my salvation be exulted,
may the name of the God of Jacob,
defend you,
may He send His help out of the sanctuary,
and strengthen you out of Zion,
may the Lord fulfill all of your petitions.

The earth is the Lord's in all its fullness,
the world and all who dwell there within,
for He has founded it upon the seas,
and established it upon the waters,
the Lord of host,
He is the
King of Glory.
Good and upright is the Lord,
therefore He teaches sinners in the way,
the humble He guides in justice,
and the humble He teaches His way.
All the paths of the Lord,
are mercy and truth,
to such that keep His covenants,
and testimony,
the secret of the Lord,
is with those who fear Him,
and He will show them His covenants.
The Lord is my light,
and my salvation,
whom shall I fear,
the Lord is the strength of my life,
of whom shall I be afraid?
Show me thy ways,
and teach me your ways,
oh' Lord,
wait on the Lord and be of good courage,
and He shall strengthen our hearts,
the Lord is my strength and my shield.
The Lord is the saving refuge of the anointed,
the voice of the Lord is over the waters,
the God of Glory thunders,
the voice of the Lord,
is powerful,
the voice of the Lord is full of majesty,
the Lord sat enthroned at the flood,
and the Lord sits as King for ever. Amen.

53. DO WE REALLY?

Written May 2000

The song says I surrender all,
my blessed Saviour,
I surrender all, but do we truly?
We sing I take this world and its earthly goods,
and I lay them at your feet,
but how about ourselves,
do we give ourselves as a living sacrifice,
holy and acceptable unto the Lord,
as our reasonable service?
Have we only given Him that,
which we have no control over,
and keep that which we think we can handle?
Looking unto the Lord where comes my help,
does not mean only when things are going bad.
I cannot control anything;
my life is not mine anymore,
if I have truly given it to God.
When the storm comes and the sun disappears,
with darkness rolling in,
and fear and doubt assail me.
Where do I look? Where do I run?
To God or to man; I've done both.
Looking unto Christ from which cometh my help,
knowing I can do all things,
through Christ who strengthens me.
All of our needs are met in Christ Jesus to them who believe.
By His stripes, whose stripes,
by Christ's stripes we were healed.
If I be lifted up, if who be lifted up,
if Christ be lifted up He will draw all men unto Himself.

I am the way-the truth, and the life,
which is the way-the truth, and the life;
Christ is the way-the truth, and the life.
Oh' yes, it is wonderful to have that trust in the Lord,
but there is a process to be that finished work,
and to be that vessel that God can use.
When we sing "Have thine own way Lord,
have thine own way",
do we really mean it?
have we counted the cost?
Look what Jesus paid.
There is hurt,
and pain in the chipping away of self,
but only for a moment compared to the eternal wait of Glory in Christ
Jesus.
There is light in the darkness and peace in the storm,
and strength in saying not my will,
but thine is born,
When we truly mean I surrender all and have thy own way.
To be built up we must be broke down first,
to be born again we must die out to self first,
to be a new creature in Christ Jesus,
old things must pass away,
then we can truly say it is no longer I,
but the Christ in me having His way.
We only have a battle when we refuse to let go, and take our hands off,
and insist in telling the potter how to do His job,
instead of saying have thine own way,
have thine own way,
for thou art the potter and I am the clay.
Lord, thou knowest and everything is in thy hands,
if we would only leave it there. Amen.

54. THE WAY

Written May, 2000.

I set out on the road of life a long long time ago,
and like a ship on the sea,
I was tossed to and fro.

I groped my way down the lane like a man blind,
but still the void was left unfilled, look here, look there self cried.
Try this; try that, one size fits all, no glimmer of light just walls.

Then one day like a whisper on the wind was God so loved the world-
that He gave His only begotten Son for all men.
Still in darkness all around, there was a light up ahead, for Jesus-Christ,
the Lamb of God is the way, He said.

I stumbled out into the light, my garment filled with stains,
but Jesus Christ the Lamb of God,
took on himself, my pain.

I went up to this wooden cross, and kneeled there at its base,
I looked upon Jesus Christ, the one who took my place.
He washed me clean from all my sins, abide His word, my
heart within.

Jesus is the way, the truth, and the life;
His word is a two edged sword,
sharper then any single edged knife. Amen.

55. WHICH ARE WE?

Written May 2000

The Bible asks these questions of man:
which do you choose?
Good or evil,
light or dark,
full of wisdom, or foolish in your ways?
Are you a worm or a butterfly,
sheep or goats,
a flock of sparrows or an eagle flying high in the sky?
Are you wheat or tares,
earthly or heavenly,
baring all your burdens or casting them on Lord Jesus,
this day to stay?
Are you tossed and driven or peace being still,
truth or lie,
is your hope in Christ?
Or you denying Him and accepting a lie from the wrong guy?
Jesus is the only way,
He stands at the door,
will you give Him His say?
He died that all would be set free,
His blood was shed and it cleansed me.
When He died,
On the third day He rose,
now we are all set free who come to Him. Amen.

56. LIGHT IN A DARKENED LAND

Written May 2000

Come to the cross where Jesus hung;
He is God's only begotten Son.
He is the bridge between man and God;
He died and rose fulfilling the law.
His blood was shed for all our sins;
He washed away stains from deep within.
He sits upon His throne on high,
and helps us see Satan's lies.
If filled with His holy spirit,
evil no,
do not want to get near it.
With pure hearts and clean hands,
we shine as lights in a darkened land. Amen.

57. FOLLOWERS OF THE GREAT I AM

Written May 2000

Be as wise as a serpent;
and as gentle as a dove.
Be as light in the darkness;
and as truthful not as lies.
Be as gold not hay,
and as faithful not to betray.
Be as good not as evil,
and as gracious not as legal.
Be ye washed in the blood of the Lamb,
and as followers of the Great I Am. Amen.

58. GOD THE PATH MAKER.

Written May 2000

You set my feet on this path,
narrow is the way;
you set my feet on this path,
and here I am to stay.

You set my feet on this path,
from darkness into light;
you set my feet on this path,
from death into life.

You set my feet on this path,
hope is all around;
You set my feet on this path,
grace and peace abound.

You set my feet on this path,
and saved my soul from sin;
You set my feet on this path,
and your blood cleansed all stains from deep within.

You set my feet on this path,
rooted and grounded am I;
You set my feet on this path,
I lift Christ Jesus high. Amen.

59. OUR LOVE DIVINE

Written May 2000

He loves us with a love so strong;
He is our love divine,
He died and rose the third day,
He is our God's true vine.

He is the mighty great I Am;
Prince of Peace indeed,
the Sacrificial Lamb of God,
who shed His blood for thee.

He loves us with a love so strong;
He is our love divine,
He died and rose the third day,
He is our God's true vine.

He is the fairest of ten-thousands;
The bright and morning star,
Lord of lords and King of kings,
The Son of God who's hands and feet are scarred.

He loves us with a love so strong;
He is our love divine,
He died and rose the third day,
and He is our God's true vine. Amen.

60. GOD'S GARDEN

Written May 2000

Have you seen a garden bursting with color and life?
With roses, daisies, daffodils,
and countless more we like.
With various colors, shapes and hues,
and sweet aromas arrayed for view.
The purples, yellows, greens, blues, pinks, oranges,
and reds displayed so true.
With all the other life maintained within these garden walls.
I had to stop and catch my breath,
Oh' God I did call.
The beautiful plants are weak and fragile,
and only survive because of someone's care.
That's how it is with God's love,
be fulfilled not bare.
He waters us with His holy word;
His spirit is our tie stake.
So join God's garden filled with love,
be true and real not false nor fake.
All the church is like a garden,
none being the same.
So let's open eyes-ears and hearts,
and take away the pain.
Let Jesus be the gardener and cultivate this plant.
So if,
"Greater is He that is in me than he that is in the world",
is true,
start saying,
In Christ I can; not I can't. Amen.

61. LIGHT OF MY LIFE

Written May 2000

You Lord are the light of my life,
and I will praise You forever.
You Lord are the light of my life,
and I trust and follow You.
It is no longer I but the Christ within me,
that is my life.
It is no longer I but the Christ within me,
that is my light.
It is no longer I but the Christ within me,
that is my hope.
It is no longer I but the Christ within me,
that is my strength.
It is no longer I but the Christ within me,
that is my peace.

You Lord are the light of my life,
forever and ever,
and ever and ever. Amen.

62. SOMETHING GOOD

Written May 2000

Something good is going to happen;
in Jesus Christ's name.
something good is going to happen;
speak it again and again.

Something good is going to happen;
pray it over all man.
something good is going to happen;
all throughout the land.

Something good is going to happen;
life and blessings abound.
something good is going to happen;
God's loving arms surround.

Something good is going to happen;
speak positively all the time.
something good is going to happen;
when we bring ourselves in line.

Something good is going to happen;
if God is your true vine. Amen.

63. GOOD OR BAD REPORTS

Written May 2000

The weatherman on the news station spoke of rain today.
I like my weatherman's reports better,
full of sunlight day by day.

The newscaster's voice drowned on and on,
bad news here bad news there,
bad news everywhere.

But there is good news His name is God,
broad casting abundant life and light for every one who comes to Him.

Though we all must decide whether or not to listen to good news or bad,
walking in the light with God or the dark with the devil.

Choosing life or death,
peace or war,
abundance or lack,
fulfillment or emptiness.

God's own son Jesus Christ,
the Blameless Lamb of God,
gave Himself-His own life,
no loss for He won. Amen.

64. SHINE ON ME

Written June 2000

Holy precious Son,
shine on me;
Holy son shine down on me,
You are the only one that I need,
Holy precious Son,
shine down on me.

Precious Holy Ghost,
reign in me;
Precious Holy Ghost,
reign in me,
Jesus sent you down to live in thee,
precious Holy Ghost,
reign in me.

Precious Holy Ghost,
cleanse me from within;
Precious Holy Ghost,
cleanse me from within,
wash me,
clean me,
purify me from all sin,
precious Holy Ghost,
cleanse me from within. Amen.

65. EVER THE SAME

Written June, 2000

Down in the valley or on a mountaintop high,
we will look to Jesus who is always nigh.

Lift up your face and call on His name,
our Jesus Lord and Saviour is ever the same,
glory hallelujah blessed be His name,
our Jesus Lord and Saviour is ever the same.

Through the stormy seas,
walking on the land shod dry,
I will look to Jesus who is always nigh,
lift up your voice and call on His name,
our Jesus Lord and Saviour is ever the same,
glory hallelujah blessed be His name,
our Jesus Lord and Saviour is ever the same. Amen.

66. LET YOUR GLORY SHOW THROUGH ME

Written June 2000

Thy beauty is not in that car outside,
nor is it in how much money you have in the bank.
Thy beauty is in thy walk with God,
the closer you walk with Him,
the more it shows.

Father let Your glory show through me,
Blessed be your name,
let Your love flow through me,
You are forever the same,
Let Your glory show through me.

Thy beauty comes not from that real nice house,
or the clothes upon your back.
Thy beauty is in thy walk with God,
the closer you walk with Him,
the more it shows.

Father let your glory show through me,
blessed be your name,
let your love flow through me,
you are forever the same,
let your glory show through me.

Thy beauty is not in how we live,
or in how many diamonds or how much gold we can display.
Thy beauty is in thy walk with God,
the closer we walk with Him,
the more it shows,

Father let thy glory show through me,
blessed be thy name,
let thy love flow through me,
you are forever the same,
let thy glory show through me.

Father let thy glory show through me,
blessed be your name,
let thy love flow through me,
you are forever the same,
let thy glory show through me. Amen.

67. THE BRIDE

Written June 2000

As I awoke I kneeled and prayed on what had been seen.
There was a bridegroom in all His splendor,
waiting for His bride to be.
His countenance glowed with anticipation,
waiting His bride to see.
The music started playing and everyone turned to glimpse the bride.
What stood there waiting to come up the aisle,
was far from what she should be.
Her dress was wrinkled and full of spots,
and the hem was uneven with little tears all around.
Her shoes were very run down at the heels,
and stained with muck and mire,
one strap held on by a pin,
the other one flapping loose.
Her veil had rends and wrinkles all around,
with hair that hung down limply,
stringy and dirty besides.
She carried flowers faded and crushed,
with a Bible with its pages missing.
With row after row of:
pearls, diamonds, emeralds, rubies, sapphires,
and gold weighing her down.
No, no, no, no!

Please do not present yourself to the bridegroom this way,
He deserves the best there is to give,
He has given the very best to us,
Can't you do the same?
So remake a new wedding dress,
no spots or stains at all.
The lacy trim so nice and smooth,
and clean about it there,
so neatly in its place,
front and back-and sides.
The veil crisp-white-and smooth,
on ringlets like a crown.
The flowers held in her hands so brilliant in color,
and lovely to behold.
The Bible was covered in calf's skin,
and gold upon its leaves,
every page accounted for,
read and believed.
The shoes of white with golden heels,
and buckles on each strap,
they fit so well and looked so good on her dainty feet.
With one single strand of pearls and gold around her slender neck,
and a pearl and gold ring to put upon her finger.

Yes, yes, yes, yes!
This is more like He deserves,
the best that we can offer,
but this one and not the first,
our time is drawing nigh,
and the Bride Groom is waiting for His Bride. Amen.

68. WORK OF THE ARTIST

Written June 2000

I thank You for the colors,
that You have painted across the sky.
The brilliant blues and soft hews,
that catch the eye.
The rosy reds, salmon pinks and scarlet,
that surprise.
The whitish gold through to bronze,
there and back again.
The softest grays or fluffiest whites,
or darkened black of dark night.
There is beauty in all its faces,
stop and take a moment or two,
to appreciate the work of the artist.
Thank You for these masterpieces,
that change from moment to moment,
and are hardly ever the same. Amen.

69. OUT OF THE WILDERNESS

Written June 2000

Going through the wilderness,
up and down I go,
blocks here and there,
going good then WOW!
Sometimes the way is smooth and straight,
at other times it is rough to go.
Beware the traps and pitfalls,
all along the way.
Sometimes you can see them afar off,
sometimes one more step and it's too late.
I am trying to go one step at a time,
checking my direction often.
No matter how smooth or rough it is,
I am assured of making it through these wilderness places,
with Jesus with me all the way.
I am coming out of this wilderness,
one step at a time;
I am coming out of this wilderness,
with Lord Jesus by my side. Amen.

70. THEY COME TO PASS

Written June 2000

The storms of life,
they come-to pass,
they mumble and grumble with flashes of light.

The wind picks up the rain comes down,
and the skies they turn dark before it is night.

Life storms shall try to over throw us,
but hold on to the cross.

Jesus Christ from whom our strength comes WON!
there is no loss.

The storms of life come,
too pass away,
with uttering and mutterings and threatening of what may come,
but this too will pass away. Amen.

71. IS GOD REALLY THERE?

Written July 2000

The lines and shapes were fetching,
the dazzle and glitter of reflecting lights blinds the eyes,
and beckons all draw nigh.
Looking into the windows that showed the true heart of man,
I am sad to say,
I saw no light only darkness deep within.
Is God really there-NO!
The beauty-the pleasure,
the dazzle of reflected light all a trap for the soul,
to those who do not know.

The next place I came upon,
was gentle in its ways,
it had a beauty but not the same.
It's lines and shapes were soft and kind,
warmth filled every corner.
This dwelling place it flowed with peace,
as I looked through the windows of this man's heart.
The glow of light from deep with in caused me to shout with glee,
and jump for joy.
Is God really there my heart tried to sing?
Yes-behold the royal ring. Amen.

72. GO AND SIN NO MORE

Written July 2000

With eyes down cast,
weak with fear,
hopelessness and despair filling her mind.
Forced to stand in the mist of them,
and this man they called Lord.
What has she done? why was she there?
Master, "this woman was taken in adultery".
The men held stones in their hands;
waiting for the Master to speak,
While He was writing something in the dirt at their feet.
He spoke at last,
saying these words to all the men there.
"He without sin may cast the first stone",
was simply all He said.
One by one they dropped their stones,
turned and walked away.
Not one remained of those who came;
only He and the woman were left.
He paused His writing in the dirt,
and asked,
"woman have you no accusers"?
With a voice filled with shame,
the woman said,
"No Lord-none remained".
With loved filled eyes He looked at her and said,
"neither do I".
"Your sins have been forgiven you,
go and sin no more".
With tear filled eyes and a grateful heart,
she went away saying,
"Truly He is the Lord". Amen.

73. MY LIGHTHOUSE

Written July 2000

My lighthouse was placed on the rocky shore,
built a long-long time ago.

Its light is seen from miles away,
telling ships caution-stay away,
while also saying safe harbor is near.

Storms may toss us to and fro,
but the light from my lighthouse is ever faithful to bring us in.

A light in the darkness that will never go out,
my safe harbor in time of trouble,
and my lifeline.

When doubts and fears seek to over throw me,
My God-Lord Jesus Christ,
is my lighthouse,
my safe harbor,
my lifeline,
and a bridge to my Father.

Our God who holds us in His hands,
in His word says,
"I am a lamp unto your feet and a light unto your pathway".

God's love shines so brightly through this darkened world,
His Glory is more brilliant than the sun.

He is faithful to bring us in if we believe in Him,
and focus on Him and His light,
to bring us safely through the storms of life to our true home. Amen.

74. WHAT DID JESUS DO?

Written July 2000

We wear leather on our wrists that says "What Would Jesus Do"?
Well why not ask "What Did Jesus Do",
for you and me.
He healed the broken hearted and He made the blind to see.
He made the lame to walk again and He set the captives free.
He turned the water into wine and He calmed the troubled seas.
He spoke this world into existence and His words caused devils to flee.
He walked upon water and He healed a withered hand.
He straightened a woman's back and tried to share His Father's plan.
Jesus said "I do nothing that I do not see my Father do";
So He came to this earth as man,
to live-learn-be obedient,
and prepare to die as God's Sacrificial Lamb.
Coming forth resurrected on the third day in victory not to stay.
This is not even half of what Jesus did,
before He ascended in the clouds back up to heaven,
to sit on the right hand of His Father,
to God be the Glory. Amen.

75. THE LETTER

Written July 2000

Dearest Love,
my Life,
my everything.

As I awoke I thought of You rejoicing in another beautiful day.
The beauty is not in the day itself but is in You my Beloved
The bird's song sounds so much happier,
now that I know that I am truly yours,
and you are truly mine.

Oh' My Love,
my life is in you,
who shed your blood for me.
Laying down your innocent life,
you died and took my place.

Oh' Joy of my Heart,
for hanging the sun-the moon and the stars for me.
My Life I gladly share with all mankind,
and rejoice with those who choose to follow after You,
Love-joy,
and peace with mercy and good besides,
following after You,
The King of kings and Lord of Lords is calling for you to come, too,
and with great Love from one in the body of Christ,
I Love You, too. Amen.

76. DAY BY DAY

Written July 2000

Lead me Lord all the way;
Lead me Lord day by day.
Lead me Lord high and low;
Lead me Lord where I must go.

Take me Lord this I pray;
Take me Lord day by day.
Take me Lord from beginning to end;
Take me Lord who is my friend.

Keep me Lord in thy sight;
Keep me Lord through the night.
Keep me Lord day by day;
Keep me Lord this I pray.

Show me Lord what is your will;
Show me Lord how to be still.
Show me Lord why do we stay;
Show me Lord this I pray.

Lead me Lord and I will follow;
Take me Lord to truth and I will swallow.
Keep me Lord in all my ways;
Show me Lord day by day I pray. Amen.

77. FOLLOW ME

Written August 2000

To walk in the light,
we needs follow the sun;
To keep in His light,
we needs follow His Son.

Jesus said "I am the way-the truth and the life,
And no one cometh unto the Father,
lest He cometh through me".
So come unto Me and I will give you rest,
to run a race and win at the end,
there is a prize And winning at the end heaven does lie.

Jesus said "I am the way-the truth and the life,
no man cometh unto the Father,
lest He cometh through me",
so come unto Me and I will give you rest.

A leader leads and bids us follow thee,
bringing all into bondage,
this leader leads and bids us follow me,
being set free in victory.

And Jesus said "I am the way-the truth and the life,
no man cometh unto the Father,
lest He cometh through Me",
So come unto Me and I will give you rest,
sayeth The Lord Jesus,
Follow Me and be set free. Amen.

78. CONSUME THE OLD

Written August 2000

The last are first and the first are last,
what is old is in the past.
From faith to faith and glory to glory,
Jesus Christ has completed one story.

Behold Jesus Christ came forth in life from death,
in power and victory.

When Jesus Christ went up to heaven on high,
God's Holy Spirit came as man's tie.
With a long distance connection between heaven and earth,
we are always plugged in when He is at work.

From faith to faith and glory to glory,
we look ahead for the beginning of the newest story.
When the Bride and the Spirit bids us come,
Jesus' final battle is already won.

Setting up His kingdom ruling with a rod of iron in His hand,
The King of kings is in His attire.
Greater thus do you than I
Holy Spirit open our eyes.
Guide us-lead us and teach us we pray,
speak to the Father thou knowest the way.

Like a firestorm sweeping across this land,
consume the old and change this man. Amen.

79. MY PRECIOUS GIFT

Written August 2000

These are the lies that bombard us all through out our lives:
You are unwanted-an accident-a mistake,
you are ugly-you are dumb-you are stupid-you are lazy,
you are good for nothing-you will never do anything right,
you won't amount to anything-you are a failure and no one can love you.

Thank God that these are all lies.
There are probably more that have not been mentioned,
but just throw them in with the rest.
Let's tear down that which destroys,
defeats and is critical,
for this is not of God.

All that God is:
Healing-renewing-a rebuilding-cleaning up,
Loving-strengthening-empowering-our hope-our resting place,
the peace that passes all understanding and so much more that is Good.

I thank God for His only begotten Son,
that He gave and I thank God,
for His Son who gave His life.

God's Love had been my precious gift,
a lifeline in the time of stormy seas,
a solid foundation on which to stand.

Let God's love take away all the hurt,
the pain-the sorrow-bitterness-the anger-the tears and the hopelessness.
Instead let God fill you with Love-Peace-Joy-Long Suffering
-Goodness-Gentleness-Meekness-Temperance and Faith.

When we make God our everything,
and say that we can do nothing of ourselves,
then we can rejoice and truly say,
of a truth God's Love is my precious gift. Amen.

80. WHICH PATH?

Written August, 2000

We all are on a path walking towards a goal,
Some are ahead-some are behind and some are walking beside us,
though we may not even know.

This path is rough,
here and there,
it is also smooth without cares.
There are wildernesses-deserts-valleys and mountain top highs,
there are road blocks-pit falls and snares that try to snare,
there are detours-side roads and short cuts galore.

It is our decision to follow Christ,
or be driven tossed to and fro;
it is our decision to lay down our own life
and picking up the cross to follow Him,
or to eat-drink and be merry for tomorrow we may die,
then spend eternity in Hell.

So on which path do you walk,
the slight path or the right path,
the old path or the bold path,
the spare all or the narrow path,
the laid back path or the take it back path,
and the last but not least,
the me path or the free path.

We are all on a path walking towards a goal,
Some are ahead-some are behind and some are walking by our side,
though we may not even know. Amen.

81. CAN YOU ENDURE?

Written September, 2000

Like the snail in the grass inching his way along,
he goes past,
one blade, two blades, now three blades of grass, Hurrah!

He is small and very slow,
but when he starts,
he goes, goes, and goes.

A beaver searches for a pleasant place and makes himself a pond.
He builds himself a dam across a creek and makes himself a home,
with twigs, branches, mud and logs,
a safe harbor from a storm.

Can we climb a mountain without taking the first step;
can we catch a fish without first setting the net?

Can we count the stars if we open not our eyes;
Can we swim the river if we don't even try?

Can our hopes come true if we don't even dream;
Can we expect to win the race when we haven't even taken the first step?

Run the race with patience enduring the cross,
some day to know and be sure in gain not loss.
Pressing on towards the mark to the high calling of God,
don't look back press on forward,
finish the race that you have begun,
continue in the race don't give up,
Heaven's crown is your loving cup. Amen.

82. ONE LOST SHEEP

Written September 2000

The Shepherd left the ninety-nine looking for one lost sheep.
The Shepherd left the ninety-nine when He heard it cry, help me!

The sheep they know the master's voice,
He calls them one by one.
The sheep they know the master's voice,
from an others they will run.

He leads them to the sweet-sweet grass and quiet flowing stream;
He is with them day and night a guard from their enemies.

The Shepherd is Jesus Christ-the Son of God indeed.
The sacrificial Lamb of God that shed His blood for thee,
who died and rose the third day,
now lives in me you see.

I was a sheep outside the fold;
the Shepherd left to find.
The shepherd's voice I now know and follow where He leads,
to sweet-sweet green grass and quiet flowing streams,
He knows just what I need. Amen.

83. PREPARE, WATCH AND WAIT

Written September 2000

My knapsack on my back,
my sword at by side,
my head gear on my head,
and Lord Jesus as my guide.

Putting on the breastplate of righteousness,
being gird about the loins with truth,
and being shod with the preparation of the gospel of peace upon my
feet.

The author and finisher of our faith,
Jesus lights the way,
through night or day.

The clarion call to one and all,
in God's mighty army,
be wakeful and watchful,
and work toward the day when our Commander in Chief comes back.

We triumph over the enemy,
through God's Son in ourselves are weak,
in Him are strong,
for God's Son won! Amen.

84. THE KEEPSAKE

Written September 2000

I was cleaning out my attic full of our past life.
There were bits of this and parts of that,
and things from long-long ago.

I slowly went through all there was cleaning as I went along.
There were bits of this and parts of that,
and things from long-long ago.

I found a box hidden under years and years of time.
There are bits of this and parts of that,
and things from long-long ago.

In this box was placed something so divine and wonderful to behold.
There is a bit of this and a part of that,
and something from long-long ago.

I found a cross, crown and robe among these books pages,
I found this keepsake among our past life,
I treasure this keepsake for it gave me life.
With a bit of this and a part of that,
and something from long-long ago. Amen.

85. DO NOT PITY ME

Written September 2000

Don't Pity Me.
Just because my eyes don't see as yours do;
Just because my ears fail to hear the tune.
Just because my mind is slow to grasp thoughts;
Just because my legs don't work for me anymore.
Just because my voice is as silent as the tomb.
Don't pity me.
If I am my Fathers child,
don't pity me,
it's nothing like a trial.
Do not pity me or my lack,
for all are lacking something.
One day I will see my Saviour's face;
I will hear His sweet voice.
I will grasp His Holy Word;
I will walk in His ways.
I will sing, worship, and praise.
So do not pity me I pray,
for all is well in God this day;
Do not pity me I pray,
for here I am in God to stay.
My Fathers hand is here to stay and complete His plan,
come what may. Amen.

86. THE CANDLE

Written September 2000

A candles flame makes a light in a darkened land.
Keep your candle burning bright,
all through out the land.
We are in Christ Jesus and Christ Jesus is in us saying,
"I am a light unto thy feet and a lamp unto thy pathway".

So the candle light keep it burning pure-clean and bright.
Let nothing quench the candles flame and leave us in the night.
Keep your candle burning bright,
a source of light in the dark of night. Amen.

87. A CHILD.

Written September 2000

Train up a child in the way it should go and when it gets old,
it shall not depart.
Train up a child in the way it should go,
for you have someone more precious than gold.

Be as a child with trust and faith,
believing our Saviour and walking in His ways.
Be as a child with trust and faith,
believing that our Saviour took our place.

Train up a child in the way they should go and when God calls,
they will follow.
Train up a child in the way it should go that when the world opens its
mouth,
it shall not swallow them whole.

You are wonderfully and fearfully made,
and the Apple of my eye God said.
You my child are precious to me,
no accident or mistake to me and that's no lie.

Train up a child in the way it should go and when it gets old,
it shall not depart.
Train up a child in the way it should go for you are so precious to my
heart. Amen.

88. I AM

Written October 2000

Jesus is the Great I Am,
in Him I am renewed.
I am the apple of God's eye;
I am precious in his sight.
I am the very reason why,
Jesus gave His life.

Jesus is the Great I Am,
in His blood I am cleansed;
I am fearfully and wonderfully made.
I am a chosen Son of God;
I am a King and Priest on high,
for Jesus won.

Jesus is the Great I Am,
in Him I am loved and forgiven now without sin;
I am a written epistle,
I am a soldier in God's mighty plan. Amen.

89. WALK WITH ME:

Written October 2000

Walk with me hand-in-hand,
and face-to-face,
walk with me oh' My Lord,
great is your grace.
I'm in You and You're in me,
together we will stand victoriously,
oh' My Lord great is Your grace.

Walk with me through day and night,
walk with me my hope of hopes and light of lights,
walk with me oh' My Lord,
great is Your grace my life's delight.
I'm in You and You are in me,
together we will stand victoriously,
oh' My Lord great is Your grace.

Walk with me till eternity reigns,
Walk with me heart-to-heart,
and name-to-name,
walk with me oh' My Lord You are forever the same.

I'm in You and You are in me,
together we will stand victoriously,
oh' My Lord great is Your grace. Amen.

90. A FRIEND, A BROTHER, A LORD

Written October 2000

A friend sticketh closer than a brother;
A friend goeth one more than due.
A friend giveth something for nothing;
A friend is Jesus Christ and a lot more,
for you and me He is the Door.

A brother cares enough to say "whoa";
A brother picks you up when you fall.
A brother keeps you in prayer;
A brother is Jesus Christ who laid down His life for thee,
that in Him there is hope galore.

A Lord knows who is His;
A Lord keeps His hand in the mist.
A Lord protects both day and night;
The Lord is Jesus Christ who won the right after winning the fight.
Amen.

91. TRUTH

Written October 2000

Truth, truth, truth;
truth will set you free.
Truth, truth, truth;
speak truth, not lie, and be at peace.
Truth, truth, truth;
Pointing out that Jesus is the way.
Truth, truth, truth;
truth, not lie, will enter the gate.
When someone asks you "did you do that",
don't give the devil anymore ground,
back him up and make him frown.
Refuse to tell another lie,
let God's truth be your guide.
Truth, truth, truth;
truth is chosen from day to day.
Truth, truth, truth;
telling lies does not pay.
Truth, truth, truth;
is the way that I will go.
Truth, truth, truth;
truth or lie, God will know any way.
When someone asks you to lie for them,
and it doesn't seem like such a big deal;
Say "NO", then pray that God will reveal the way.
Lies are nothing but Satan's traps,
get in to God's word and follow His maps.
Truth, truth, truth;
it rules, its phat, it flies.
Truth, truth, truth;
live for truth and death to lies.
Truth, truth, truth;
that is who Jesus is and that's no lie.
Truth, truth, truth;
truth is your best friend, so choose for the right. Amen.

92. WRAP OUR TREASURES IN TRUTH

Written October 2000

We have treasures here on earth,
young minds to shape and mold.
I take this honor deeply to heart,
benefits unbound are bestowed.
These treasures should be handled with love,
and care and truth at every turn.
We break them down to make them simple,
and sometimes loose truth along the way.
Then young minds receive less them all,
to carry them day by day.
Then we wonder why Mary said this,
and Johnny repeated something different,
supposedly the same.
This is one way the enemy defeats,
with questions that cause us to doubt.
So let us keep it simple but true to God's word,
and wrap our treasures with things that don't,
rust, spoil or decay. Amen.

93. WOULD YOU DO THAT IF JESUS WERE STANDING BY?

Written October 2000

Take a stool;
Bend an elbow,
that won't matter.
Who cares,
No one you know comes here anyway.
Did you give your life to Jesus Christ,
would you do that if He were standing by?

Speaking things that belong in the trash,
or down in the gutter with the sewage,
is that how Jesus spoke.
Would you do that if Jesus were standing by?

Push, shove and kick till they bleed,
for they don't live like you and me,
is that what Jesus taught when He walked upon this earth.
Would you do that if Jesus were standing by?

Well guess what He is!
So please before you do think or speak,
ask this question of yourself,
would I do this if Jesus Christ were standing by?
If not, "don't". Amen.

94. DON'T FEEL SORRY FOR ME

Written October 2000

My eyes may miss more of what you see,
but please don't feel sorry for me;
I may not see your lovely face,
or tell the color of your hair,
but God has blessed me with color and light,
I wish that I could share.

Even in the darkest room it is not dark to me,
for God has given me color and light beautiful to see,
So please do not feel sorry for me,
I would God's beauty you would see.

My eye may miss some beauty here on earth,
but God's glorious light I count much more worth. Amen.

95. NAIL PIERCED HANDS

Written October 2000

My Lord, my Saviour, my Jesus Christ,
with tear washed feet that were hair dried,
not long before they were nail pierced besides.

The Son of God who became a man and walked upon this earth,
healing and blessing and doing good and much more than we deserved.

Thank You Lord Jesus Christ for taking my place,
and shedding Your blood for me,
with a thorn pierced brow-and broken body and nail pierced hands and
nail pierced feet,
Your love has set me free.

I am thankful to the woman,
who washed Your feet with her tears,
and dried them with her hair,
for she was there and I was not,
to take such care of thee.
I love You my Lord, my Saviour, my Jesus Christ, and my King.
I am grateful for God's plan that had You take my place,
for this I could not face.
The thorn pierced brow-the broken body, the nail pierced hands and nail
pierced feet,
all for me
You took my place and shed Your blood for thee. Amen.

96. SEASONS COME AND SEASONS GO

Written—October 2000.

The eagle flies into the sun;
Children laugh while having fun.
Seasons come and seasons go;
I hope one day that you will know,
you are loved by Jesus so.

Like the eagle that flies into the sun face,
I pray for you God's mercy, power, and grace.
Seasons come and seasons go;
I hope someday that you will know,
you are loved by Jesus so.

Like the river that flows to the sea,
God's Son died for you and me.
Seasons come and seasons go;
My hope for you is that one day you will know,
that Jesus died to set you free and all His blood was shed for thee.
Amen.

97. IN GOD'S TIME

Written November 2000

Like the stars up in the sky or the sands upon the beach,
we know not our time till it is reached.

These days look dark,
but that won't last in God's time His kingdom will come to pass.
One day soon we will look up,
and see Jesus coming in the clouds.

Looking up to Him from which cometh our strength,
our rock, our shield, our peace and our grace.

These days look dark but that won't last;
soon Jesus' Kingdom shall come to pass. Amen.

98. MAKING THIS PART WHOLE

Written November, 2000

A journey starts with just one step;
a fire starts with just one spark,
The narrow path is in the light;
the wide path is in the dark.

A garden starts with just one seed;
a poem starts with just one mark,
I thank You Lord Jesus Christ,
Saviour of my soul;
I thank You Lord Jesus Christ for making this part whole.

Take up your cross and follow me said Jesus Christ our King,
take up your cross and follow me,
and gain your crown, robe, and ring.

A symphony starts with just one note,
porridge starts with just one oat,
I thank You Lord Jesus Christ Saviour of my soul;
I thank You Lord Jesus Christ for making this part whole.

a color starts with just one hue,
a rainbow starts with just one drop of dew,
Take up your cross and follow me said Jesus Christ our King,
take up your cross and follow me,
and gain your crown, robe, and ring. Amen.

99. THE PORTRAIT GALLERY

Written November 2000

This gallery of portraits hanging on the wall,
is a portrayal of life with man's victorious ascent or downward fall,
with or without God.

The first is a portrait of a Sheperd,
watching carefully after His sheep.
This second one portrays a wolf among the sheep,
scattered to and fro.
The third portrays a beggar wounded, neglected and sore at the gate.
Now this fourth one you see is Jesus at the well,
the Living Water, for you and me.
Looking on the fifth one we see Jesus nailed to the tree,
giving His life's blood to cleanse us from all sin,
setting us free.
In the sixth portrait hanging there is a serpent under feet,
in which our Lord and Saviour took from him the keys.
The seventh portrait hanging on the wall is a black, black open maw,
follow after Jesus and in there you won't fall.
The last portraying mans life, is two paths;
one narrow and the other wide,
the narrow path is straight away and few walk there on,
the wide path is trodden down with way to many feet to count.
At the end of the narrow path is a bridge to Heavens Gates;
Jesus is the only way to get to Heavens crown.
For those who chose the wide path, its end is Hell alone.
Choose the straight and narrow way and find peace untold.

Become a soul brought from darkness into the marvelous light,
and see God's love unfold to thee more precious than gold. Amen.

100. DRY YOUR EYES

Written November 2000

Little faces looking out windows cold as ice.
Looking for someone to come and warm their lives.

These little ones who have been left behind need more than clothes or
food,
they need someone to come and rap their arms around them, too.

Their hopeless eyes and love starved faces,
holds on to anyone who pays them attention that is nice.

With tear-stained faces and love-starved hearts,
they cry out to be loved and a part.

These children who have been left behind,
need some one's loved filled heart.

So dry your eyes and know that Jesus wants to draw near.

He wants to fill your empty places;
He wants to heal your wounded spaces.

So dry your eyes and let Him draw near.
Bringing you out of the darkest despair,
to a loving hope filled life so rare.

Jesus loves you so much,
Why don't you let Him show you how much? Amen.

101. ONLY ONE

Written November 2000

It only takes one spark to get a fire going.
It only takes one mark to get a novel flowing.

It only takes one moment and time has passed away.
It only takes one note and a symphony is played.

It only took one name to free the heavy hearted.
It only took one action and the Red Sea parted.

It only took one grain of sand to make a matchless pearl.
It only took the life of one man to free an entire world.

Jesus is the only man who lived and died for me.
Jesus is the only one who shed His blood for thee.

Jesus is the only one who died and lives again.
Jesus is the only one who freed us from sin.

The prince of darkness where lays all that is evil.
He comes to lie, steal, and destroy many a life along the way.

He would, that you thought that he were the only one to give you your
heart's cry.
But all you get is dark despair and agony the rest of your eternal life.

So turn to the only one who died and lives again.
Jesus Christ, the Lamb of God,
who takes away our sins. Amen.

102. GOD'S RAINBOW ON LAND

Written January 2001.

To hands that grasp and link in love and prayer,
in faith and joy or in sorrow and tears.
I love God's work and all He has done upon this earth,
and in those He can complete His plan.
Just like the tiny grains of sand,
we are multi colored like a rainbow on land.
There are no divisions beyond the pearly gates;
there are no segregated lots for us to take.
No Baptists, no Methodists, no Jew, we are all God's children,
He created you too.
Black and White, Red and Yellow and Brown stand side by side,
we do not see the color of the skin,
but what is deep inside.
Put on blinders when it comes to the skin of the neighbors who live
beside us,
be color blind when it comes to the skin,
for it is what is deep inside that counts with Christ.
For all of those who come putting our in His,
being linked with our Lord and Saviour who is linked with our Father
God on high.
We are all together in God's garden,
brilliant colors galore.
Do not judge this book by its cover, you do not know what is in store,
read the pages that are within and see the story unfold.
A piece of coal when brought from the ground is chipped away at and
broke,
for it hides a precious stone when polished is dazzling in the light.
Let God show what is within the heart of your fellow man,
and see God's love, mercy and grace to fulfill His Holy plan for you and
me. Amen.

103. THE MAN

Written February 2001

Long, long ago and far away,
there was a man who died one day,
upon a cross on a hill shedding His blood and making God real.

The man who died upon that cross,
was God's own son who came to save the lost.

He died to set the captives free,
but that's not all He did for you and me.

On the third day He rose again,
conquering sin, death, hell and the grave for all men.

He took our place who knew no sin,
His precious blood washes us deep within.

Jesus was the bridge between man and God;
to bring Grace, mercy and peace for soul sake,
from God who sent Him,
who fulfilled the law.

Jesus was the bridge between man and God;
to bring Grace, mercy and peace for soul sake,
from God who sent Him, who fulfilled the law.

He left promising to return again,
to gather the wheat from the harvest into His barns.

King Jesus will rule with a rod of iron in His hand,
setting up His Kingdom for His thousand-year reign in this land.

There is no end to this story from long, long ago,
watch and see it unfold pure as gold. Amen.

104. O'LORD JESUS, HOW I LOVE YOU

Written February 2001

O Lord Jesus how I love You, need and adore You.
You are everything to me,
You are my life.

O Lord Jesus how I love You, need and adore You.
You are beautiful, wonderful and marvelous to see.

O Lord Jesus how I do love You, need and adore You,
My life is in You, with peace and joy, too.

O Lord Jesus how I love You,
You are beautiful, wonderful and marvelous to me.

When I am lost in You I am found.
When I am tossed in You I am sound.

O Lord Jesus how I love You,
You are beautiful, wonderful and marvelous to me.

My Lord Jesus how I love You,
You are beautiful, wonderful and marvelous to me. Amen.

105. STANDING ON THE ROCK, CHRIST JESUS

Written February 2001

Standing on the Rock Christ Jesus,
the stone the builders disallowed.
Standing on the Rock Christ Jesus,
look at where He is now.
Standing on the Rock Christ Jesus,
no storm nor wave bring low.
Standing on the Rock Christ Jesus,
secure in all we know.
Standing on the Rock Christ Jesus,
rooted and grounded to stay.
Standing on the Rock Christ Jesus,
His life for us He paid. Amen.

106. YOU LORD JESUS

Written February 2001

You Lord Jesus are the Lovely Rose of Sharon,
whose fiery red peddles seemed bathed in golden light.
You Lord Jesus are the Bright and Morning Star,
who while we are in praise,
dances over us near and far.
You Lord Jesus are the Prince of Peace,
whose love and forgiveness brings men to their knees.
You Lord Jesus are the Christ,
who took on our sins and bore our stripes.
You Lord Jesus are the Lamb of God,
who died for us and came forth in resurrected life, not death. Amen.

107. SETTING ME FREE

Written February 2001

Like a spring that bubbles up in a dry and thirsty land,
You are the water that quenches this thirsty man.
You are the water that flows from God's own throne,
and who ever drinks there,
will never thirst no more.

Like a man starved for more than man supplies,
You are the bread that keeps this man alive.
Your Holy Word fills this man inside,
You are the word of truth and not of lie.

Jesus is God's son,
who came and took our place;
Christ is the one,
who will come again one day,
and take His church away.

Thank You Lord for bearing all for me,
Your precious blood was shed and set me free.
Your precious blood was shed and set me free,
now I am clean. Amen.

108. THE ONE AND THE ONLY WAY

Written February 2001

Jesus is the one and the only way,
Jesus is the life I live today.
Jesus is the Word and the Lamb of God;
Jesus is the Prince of Peace that surpasses all we know.

Jesus is the Joy down within my heart;
Jesus' blood has washed me clean white as snow.
Jesus is the One and the only Way,
Jesus is the Life I live today. Amen.

109. PUTTING ON MY SOLDIER'S GARB

Written February 2001

Putting on my soldier's garb,
preparing for war. Reading in my warfare manual,
taking stock of what's in store.

On the training ground day and night,
trusting in my Commander-in-Chief.
Putting on my soldier's garb,
shod with the Gospel of Peace.

Putting on my breast plate of righteousness,
guarding what lies beneath,
to this we add also the belt of Truth,
without that I will not speak.

The helmet covering my mind protects it from the enemies sneak
attacks.
I hold my shield upon my arm to drive the fiery darts back.

Last but not least,
The sword of the Spirit is the weapon I choose to use.
Faithfully reading that warfare manual is showing me,
in Christ I do not lose.

Putting on my soldier's garb,
preparing for the war,
the enemy thinks that he has won,
though in Christ Jesus,
we know that he has lost forever more. Amen.

110. MORE THAN ONE TASTE

Written February 2001

Don't be caught sleeping when Jesus returns,
work out your salvation for the Kingdom to learn.

Seeking and searching for God's Holy Face,
Thirsting and hungering for more than one taste.

Wash me clean whiter than snow,
O God, You are faithful this I do know.

Thank You O God for taking our place,
the things that You bore,
I know I could not face.

Your mercy and grace and Holy Name,
I thank You O God,
for You are ever the same. Amen.

111. O'LORD JESUS

Written February 2001

O Lord Jesus we need You,
O Lord we need You,
we need You every day,
we need You all the way,
O Lord Jesus we need You.

O Lord Jesus we need You,
O Lord Jesus we need You,
we need You every day,
we need You all the way,
O Lord Jesus we need You. Amen.

112. REST, PEACE AND JOY

Written—February 2001

There is rest in my God,
who holds me in His hand.
There is peace in my God,
that passes all understanding.
There is joy in my God,
that springs forth from my heart,
there is rest and there is peace,
there is joy in my God,
there is rest and there is peace,
and there is joy in my God. Amen.

113. THERE IS REST, PEACE AND JOY IN MY GOD

Written February 2001

There is rest, rest,
rest in my God,
who holds me in His hand.
There is peace, peace,
peace that passes all understanding.
There is joy, joy,
joy that springs forth from my heart.
There is rest and peace and joy in my God,
there is rest and peace and joy in my God. Amen.

114. ARE YOU THE SHEPHERD'S SHEEP?

Written February 2001

Come to the well that never runs dry,
never runs dry, never runs dry,
come to the well that never runs dry and never thirst again.

Feed in the pasture lush and green,
lush and green, lush and green,
feed in the pasture lush and green with what God sets before you.

Hear the Shepherd call His sheep,
call His sheep, call His sheep,
hear the Shepherd call His sheep and bring them into the fold.

See Him count them one by one,
one by one, one by one,
see Him count them one by one to see that none are lost.

He leaves the ninety-nine to go after the one,
to go after the one, to go after the one,
He leaves the ninety-nine to go after the one and hunts for it high and
low.

Hallelujah I found my sheep,
I found my sheep, I found my sheep,
hallelujah I found my sheep He rejoices all the way home. Amen.

115. "HOSANNA"

Written February 2001

Hosanna, hosanna the people cried.
Hosanna, hosanna as Jesus did ride by.

On a young donkey He rode into Jerusalem,
as the story for told.
He could have been King,
but Jesus chose to be the sacrificial lamb,
on whom all was disposed.

He laid down His life for every man,
and rose again the Great I Am.
There was no loss dying on that tree,
He gained total victory for you and me.

For on the third day He rose again,
after saying "IT IS FINISHED",
who bore all our sins.
And now He sits as King on high,
and in Him so do I. Amen.

116. THOU SHALL HAVE NO OTHER GOD BEFORE ME

Written March 2001

Sow to yourselves in Righteousness,
reap in mercy.
Break up your fallow ground,
for it is time to seek the Lord.
Till He comes and rain righteousness upon you.
For I am God not man,
The Holy One in the mist of thee.
Therefore turn thou to thy God,
keep mercy and judgment and wait on thy God continually.
Yet I am the Lord thy God,
and thou shall know no God but Me.
For there is no Saviour besides Me.
O' Israel thou has destroyed thyself,
but in Me is help,
I will be thy King.
I will ransom them from the power of the grave;
I will redeem them from death.
O' Israel return to the Lord thy God,
for thou has fallen by thy iniquity.
Take with you words,
and turn to the Lord and say unto Him,
take away all iniquity and receive us graciously.
They that dwell under His shadow shall return.
They will revive as the corn and grow as the vine.
Who is wise and he shall understand these things,
prudent and he shall know them.
For the ways of the Lord are right,
and the just shall walk in them,
but the transgressors shall fall in them. Amen.

117. POUR OUT YOUR SPIRIT

Written March 2001

Pour out Your Spirit upon all flesh O God,
and Let our sons and daughters prophecy.
Pour out Your Spirit upon all flesh O God,
that our old men see dreams and our young men see visions.
Pour out Your Spirit upon all flesh O God,
among the servants and handmaids too.
Pour out Your Spirit upon all flesh O God,
and show wonders in the heavens and upon the earth.
Pour out Your Spirit upon all flesh O God,
and show blood, fire and pillars of smoke.
Pour out Your Spirit upon all flesh O God,
to see the sun turn to darkness and the moon to blood,
what a day that will be.
Pour out Your Spirit upon all flesh O God,
for the Great and Terrible Day of The Lord is come. Amen.

118. THE SUN SHALL CEASE TO SHINE AND THE MOON SHALL TURN TO BLOOD

Written March 2001

The Great and Terrible Day of The Lord will come to man.
The Great and Terrible day of The Lord will come to man.
The sun shall cease to shine;
the moon shall turn to blood.
The Great and Terrible Day of The Lord will come to man.

But if ye call on Jesus,
ye shall be delivered.
But if ye call on Jesus,
ye shall be saved.
Yes if ye call on Jesus,
ye shall be delivered.
Yes if ye call on Jesus,
ye shall be saved.

The Great and Terrible Day of The Lord is come to man.
The Great and Terrible Day of The Lord is come to man.
The sun shall cease to shine;
the moon shall turn to blood.
The Great and Terrible Day of The Lord is come to man.

But if ye call on Jesus,
ye shall be delivered.
But if ye call on Jesus,
ye shall be saved.
Yes if ye call on Jesus,
ye shall be delivered.
Yes if ye call on Jesus,
ye shall be saved.

The Great and Terrible Day of The Lord has come to man.
The Great and Terrible Day of The Lord has come to man.
The sun has ceased to shine;
the moon has turned to blood.
The Great and Terrible Day of The Lord has come to man.

And if ye'd called on Jesus,
ye'd been delivered.
And if ye'd called on Jesus,
ye'd been saved.
Yes if ye'd called on Jesus,
ye'd been delivered.
Yes if ye'd called on Jesus,
ye'd been saved. Amen.

119. LET THERE BE

Written March 2001

Let there be;
peace, peace, peace of God,
in this house,
let there be;
peace, peace, peace of God,
in this house,
let there be;
peace, peace, peace of God,
in this house,
for thou O' God are the Prince of Peace indeed.

Let there be;
rest, rest, rest of God,
in this house,
let there be;
rest, rest, rest of God,
in this house,
let there be;
rest, rest, rest of God,
in this house,
for thou O' God hold me in Your hand.

Let there be;
love, love, love of God,
in this house,
let there be;
love, love, love of God,
in this house,
let there be;
love, love, love of God,
in this house,
for thou O' God first Loved thee.
Let there be;
joy, joy, joy of God,
in this house,
let there be;
joy, joy, joy of God,
in this house,
let there be;
joy, joy, joy of God,
in this house,
for thou O' God I rejoiceth to see.

Let there be;
need, need, need of God,
in this house,
let there be;
need, need, need of God,
in this house,
let there be;
need, need, need of God,
in this house,
for thou O' God set the captives free in victory. Amen.

120. BE YE READY

Written March 2001

If ye are going to talk the talk,
be ye ready to walk the walk,
as our God has called us to do.

If ye are going to seek God's face,
be ye ready to kneel and earnestly pray,
as our God has called us to do.

If ye are going to walk in the light,
be ye ready to flatten fleshes fight,
as our God has called us to do.

If ye are going to take up the cross,
be ye ready to count the cost,
as our God has called us to do.

If ye are going to run the race,
be ye ready to win taking first place,
as our God has called us to do.

If ye are going to plant the seed,
be ye ready to reap, reap, reap,
as our God has called us to do.

If ye are going to live in Him,
be ye ready not to sin,
as our God has called us to do.

If ye are going to be victorious in God,
be ye ready to plead the Blood that was shed on the cross,
as our God has called us to do.

If ye are going to talk the talk,
be ye ready to walk the walk,
as our God has called us to do. Amen.

121. NOT THE END

Written April, 2001,

They laid Him in a manger's trough wrapped in swaddling clothes.
He came from His throne up above,
taking on flesh dwelling here below.
Knowing that His Father our God loved us so.

He learned and grew and became a man,
putting away childish things,
He learned and grew and became a man,
obedient in every thing.

He was the precious lamb of God,
who came and took our place;
He was the precious lamb of God,
whose blood washed our sins away.

Walking along dusty roads,
He said "Come and follow Me."
Walking along dusty roads His words set people free.

They placed Him on that wooden cross,
He bore it all for you and me,
they placed Him on that wooden cross,
He died to set all man free,
from sin, death, hell and the grave,
and live in victory.

They laid Him in a borrowed tomb,
wrapped in grave clothes.
After three days He arose in all God's glory.
He ascended on high in victory,
rejoice and praise His Holy Name,
for this is not the end of His story. Amen.

123. GOD'S LOVE

Written April, 2001,

God's love sent His Son to earth,
God's love made the way,
God's love kept Him upon that cross,
until the penalty for us He did pay.

God's love put Him in that tomb,
God's love brought Him forth again,
and God's love gave us another chance to come close to Him.

God's love brought us from death to life.
God's love brought us out of darkness into the marvelous light.
God's love brought us back to Him,
through His only begotten Son Jesus Christ.

There is no love without God's love,
there is no love without Him,
there is no love without God's love,
open your heart and welcome Him in. Amen.

124. THE FATHER OF FATHER'S WORDS

Written April, 2001

I call you righteous,
I call you holy;
I call you the anointed of God.

I call you precious,
I call you my children,
and I call you the apple of my eye.

I call you conqueror,
I call you victorious,
and I call you abundantly blessed.

I call you my body,
I call you the church,
and I call you the sheep of my fold.

I call you my lights,
I call you my written Epistles,
and I call you my vessels of gold. Amen.

125. JESUS: RIGHTEOUS, HOLY AND MIGHTY

Written April, 2001,

Jesus, Jesus, Jesus,
Jesus our holy Lord.
Jesus, Jesus, Jesus,
babe that was born.

Righteous, righteous, righteous,
righteous Lamb of God.
Righteous, righteous, righteous,
sent from above.

Holy, Holy, Holy,
Holy pure and true.
Holy, Holy, Holy,
baring all for me and you.

Mighty, Mighty, Mighty,
Mighty God indeed.
Mighty, Mighty, Mighty,
who set the captive free in victory.

Jesus, Jesus, Jesus,
Jesus our Holy Lamb of God.
Jesus, Jesus, Jesus,
who comes when He is called. Amen.

126. PRAISE YE THE LORD

Written April 2001

Praise ye the Lord, praise ye Jehovah,
praise ye the Lord, praise Your Holy Name.

Praise Ye the Lord, praise Ye Jehovah,
praise Ye the Lord, for You are forever the same.

Blessed be the Lord, blessed be Jehovah,
blessed be the Lord, blessed be Your Holy Name.

Blessed be the Lord, blessed be Jehovah,
blessed be the Lord, for You are forever the same.

Rejoice in the Lord, rejoice in Jehovah,
rejoice in the Lord, and rejoice in Your Holy Name.

Rejoice in the Lord, rejoice in Jehovah,
rejoice in the Lord, and rejoice for He is forever the same. Amen.

127. MEET MY FATHER

Written June 2001

Come let me introduce you to my Father,
and tell you something about Him.

My Father is generous in His giving,
and Holy in all His ways,
and He is merciful from day to day to day.

My Father is creative and artistic,
and He is righteous and true.

My Father sits upon His throne in a place not made by hands,
He knows all about you and I,
and every step we take.

My Father is the husbandman,
His Son is the true vine,
and He calls us, who's us,
and draws us to Himself through His Son-Jesus Christ.

My Father is God Almighty,
the one and only God is He,
He heals the broken-hearted,
He makes the blind to see,
He makes the lame to walk again,
and He sets the captives free.

My Father is God on high,
who also lives within me;
He is my fortress, my shield and buckler,
and my safe hiding place from the enemy.

My Father is the Great I Am,
who loved so much that He gave;
He won the battle over sin, death, hell and the grave,
when He came and took our place. Amen.

128. YES, FOR, YOU!

Written June 2001

You O' Lord are sweeter than the sweetest smelling rose that grows.
You O' Lord are purer than the purest driven snow.
You O' Lord are truer than the truest story ever told.
You O' Lord are the light of my life,
there is no life without you.
For you O' Lord are everything to me.
For you O' Lord are my sufficient need.
For you O' Lord guide my every step to thee.
For you O' Lord are holy and who I need.
Yes you O' Lord show me new mercies from day-to-day.
Yes you O' Lord, are my strength in my weakness, you make me strong.
Yes you O' Lord are my hope all along the way.
Yes you O' Lord are my life,
there is no life without you my God. Amen.

129. MY GOD, MY SAVIOUR, AND MY LORD

Written June 2001

There is no love like God's love.
There is no love like the Lord's.
There is no love like agape love,
John 3:16 tells us more.
There is no Father like God the Father.
There is no Son like the Lord.
There is no Spirit like the Holy Spirit,
read God's word and explore.

There is no time like the present.
There is no time to waste any more.
There is no time to look behind you.
Take time only to look to Jesus the Door.

There is no hope without Jesus.
There is no life without the Lord.
There is no Peace without the Prince of Peace,
fall on the rock and be restored. Amen.

130. GOD WILL NEVER FAIL

Written June 2001

Don't waste another minute,
don't take another step,
Don't count on more tomorrows,
for they have surely fled.
Unless Jesus is your Saviour,
unless God is your guide,
unless Jesus is your Lord,
there will be no open door,
for you and you will be denied.
So choose Jesus as Lord and Saviour,
choose God as your true guide,
choose living instead of dying,
and be a partaker of blessing and life.

Jesus is our Lord and Saviour,
there is no other way,
and God will truly guide us,
if we let Him,
but we choose the path we take.

Partake of living instead of dying,
partake of heaven instead of hell,
and partake of blessing instead of cursing,
for God Almighty will never forsake nor fail. Amen.

131. I SAY, YES!

Written June 2001

I say Yes to Christ Lord Jesus.
I say Yes to all God's ways.
I say Yes to all His commandments.
I say Yes and give You the praise.
I say Yes and give You the praise.

I say Yes to Godly living.
I say Yes to Holy ways.
I say Yes to life in Jesus.
I say Yes and give You the praise;
I say Yes and give You the praise. Amen.

132. CAN'T DO IT WITHOUT YOU!

Written June, 2001

I can't do it without You,
I can not do it alone,
I can't do it without You,
without You there is no hope.

Help me Father hold my hand,
guide me every step of the way,
help me Lord see Your plan,
and walk it day-to-day.

I can't do it without You,
I can not do it alone,
I can't do it without You,
without You Lord I am not reborn.

I can't do it without You Father,
I can not do it alone Lord,
I can't do it without you Father,
without You heaven would not be my home. Amen.

133. IF WE ONLY KNEW

Written June 2001

O' my God if we only knew the affects for good,
or evil that comes from our words and deeds.
O' God change us I plea.

Every time I put my arms around my fellow man with a Godly hug,
I am hugging a part of you O' my God.

Every time I speak good or evil of my fellow man,
I am speaking of you O' my God.

Every time I am doing something or not,
I am doing it or not unto you O' my God.

Every time I go the extra mile or not,
I am going that extra mile or not for you O' my God.

Open our eyes, ears and hearts,
and reveal to us your truths,
open our eyes, ears and hearts O' my God,
and make us more like you.

O' my God if we only knew the affects for good,
or evil that comes from our words and deeds O' my God,
what a difference there would be. Amen.

134. BATTLES

Written July 2001

I stood upon a mountain high contemplating times gone bye.
The battles on that mountain top,
those who won and those who lost.
It was not so very long ago,
I found myself in a battle so.
One of hopelessness, one of despair,
one of darkness, not wanting to be there.
I felt as if I would drown in all the troubles that were around.
Crying O' God help me I pray,
I don't know what to do,
I need You today.
The ball and chain that held me fast,
My God unlocked I was free at last.
To walk into the marvelous light,
I held God's hand and held it tight.
He broke the chains and set me free,
His loving arms surrounded me.
God the Father-God the Son,
God the Holy Spirit three in one.
Now I follow truth and light,
for in God is hope, love, joy and life. Amen.

135. SEEK GOD'S FACE AND NOT HIS HANDS

Written July 2001

To seek God's face and not His hands,
to find God's heart of love for man,
to keep God's word every step of the way in righteousness,
and truth ever willing to obey.

Looking to our Lord for strength,
He guideth every step we take.

O' worship God our mighty King,
Master over everything,
seek God's face and not His hands;
find God's heart of love for man. Amen.

136. WALK BY FAITH AND NOT BY SIGHT

Written July 2001

Walk by faith and not by sight,
peace be still all storms of the night.

Jesus is the Prince of Peace,
a lamp to light the path for our feet.
Jesus is the Son of God,
whose blood was shed for one and all.

Walk by faith and not by sight,
carry the standard of Christ's Cross high true and right.

For it's neither by might nor by power,
but by my Spirit sayeth the Lord.
So run the race set before you,
ask, seek and knock at the door,
Jesus Christ is the door and a lot more.

Walk by faith and not by sight,
firmly planted in the Rock Christ Jesus shod dry. Amen.

137. VICTORY IS WON

Written July 2001

Put on a garment of praise;
be clothed in humbleness, righteousness, purity,
steadfastness and faith.

Walk in His will,
His word and His way,
seeking not His hand but His face.

Quick to hear but slow to speak,
patient, gentle, loving and meek.

Casting all our cares on God,
think it not strange nor odd.

The battle is The Lord's,
Victory is won,
and Jesus Christ is God's Son. Amen.

138. BUILD UPON A FOUNDATION OF PRAYER

Written July, 2001

Build upon a foundation of prayer,
Speaking God's word stirs more than the air.
It sets in motion things unseen,
releasing God's power binding the enemies.

The light of God swallows the dark,
the light is God's word,
fill up your heart.
Open your mouth let it flow from your lips,
the word of God healeth all that are sick.
So build your foundation on prayer,
finding out that God is truly aware. Amen.

139. O MY GOD, I PRAY, HEAR MY PRAYER

Written July 2001

O God I pray You hear my prayer,
for total change done in me,
doing Your will gratefully.

To seek Your Face and not Your Hand,
to look to You and not to man.

To guide me and lead me in all my ways,
to strengthen me from day-to-day.

To give You control of all of me,
keeping You close Who set me free.

O My God I pray hear my prayer;
I need You and Love You,
casting on You all my cares. Amen.

140. GOD O GOD

Written July, 2001

God of wonder,
God of light,
God I need You day and night.
God of mercy,
God of grace,
God O' God let me see Your face.
God of one,
God of all,
God of creatures great and small.
God of righteousness,
God of love,
God O' God send down Your rain from above,
God of truth,
God of life,
God O' God make us holy and unified. Amen.

141. A PRAYER OF CHANGE, GUIDANCE, STRENGTH AND SAFE KEEPING

Written July 2001

Change me Lord,
from day-to-day,
in thy hand like molded clay.
Guide me Lord,
every step of the way,
in my need all is met each and every day.
Strengthen me Lord,
with thy might,
in God is the true light of life.
Keep me Lord,
in thy hand;
only in You can I stand. Amen.

142. WATCH, LOOK AND LISTEN

Written July, 2001

Watching for Our Saviours return,
Looking east from whence He will come,
Listening for the sound of a trumpet blast,
splitting the Heavens in His wake.

Dividing the land of Israel with a quake.
Setting up His Kingdom for His thousand year reign.
Rightfully ruling as the Lion of Judah,
and The Lamb that was sleighen.

Watching for our Saviour to return,
looking east from whence He will come,
Listening for the sound of the trumpet blast,
for You are the First and the Last. Amen.

143. DEAREST CHILD

Written July 2001

Dearest child close to my heart,
I love You but not what keeps us apart.
I draw You and woo You and call You my own,
but how much am I really known? You ask and seek and knock at the
door,
but all You want is more, more, more.
You would be amazed of my plans for You,
come and seek my face and try something new.
To You my child for whom much abounds,
who once was lost but now am found.
Put Me first and let Me reign,
and you My child will never be the same.
Dearest child the apple of my eye,
knowest that I am always near by.
Love Your Heavenly Father. Amen.

144. OUR GOD MOST HIGH

Written August 2001

Taste and see how good God is.
Look and see His awesomeness.
Bough before Almighty God,
who made all the heavens and the earth.

Rejoice and praise His holy name,
soaring to the sky a song of praise,
with a thank filled heart,
lifting God Almighty high.

Seek God's face and not His hands.
Choose God's holy way and not man's.
Rest in God's abiding arms and find,
hope, peace, love and strength.

Rejoice and praise His holy name,
soaring to the sky a song of praise,
from a thank filled heart,
lifting God Almighty high.

Trust that God means good for you.
Keep yourself in all His ways.
Walk in God's holy word every single day.

Rejoice and praise His holy name,
soaring to the sky a song of praise,
with a thank filled heart,
lifting up Almighty God high.

Rejoice and praise His holy name,
soaring to the sky a song of praise,
with a thank filled heart lifting up El' El' Yone,
our God Most High. Amen.

145. I CHOOSE YOU:

Written September, 2001,

I choose you, who is my all, I choose you, who is my strength, I choose you, who gave me life, I choose you, Lord-God, I choose you.

I choose you, who broke my bonds, I choose you, who bore my stripes, I choose you, who healed my wounds, I choose you, Lord-God, I choose you.

I choose you, who is my hope, I choose you, who is my joy, I choose you, who died for me, I choose you, Lord-God, I choose you.

I choose you, who is my Lord, I choose you, who is my God, I choose you, who is coming back for me, I choose you, Lord-God, Who first chose me, I now choose You. Amen.

146. FREELY, YOU GAVE

Written September 2001

Freely You gave,
gratefully I receive.
Freely You came,
joyfully I believe.

Worthy of death,
You took my place.
Worthy of Hell,
You showed me another way.

Holy You are,
in all Your ways,
Gracious and Merciful day after day.

Freely You paid in full,
as humbly I repent.
Freely You forgave,
as tearfully I ask You to forgive.

Worthy of death through Christ,
Your love gives me life.
Worthy of Hell through Christ,
Heaven is no longer denied.

Holy You are,
in all of Your ways,
Gracious and Merciful day after day.
Holy You are,
in all of Your ways,
Gracious and Merciful day after day. Amen.

147. FATHER, I THANK YOU, FOR WHO YOU ARE

Written September 2001,

Father I thank You,
Holy, Pure and True,
Father I thank You,
for who You are.
Father I praise Your name,
Holy forever the same,
Father I praise Your name,
for who You are.
Father I rejoiceth in You,
Pure, Holy and True,
Father I rejoiceth in You,
for who You are.
Father I Praise Your Name,
let all Heaven and Earth Proclaim,
Father, Praise Your Name,
for who You are.
Father I Worship You,
True, Pure and Holy, oo,
Father I Worship You,
for who You are.
Father I thank You,
Gracious, Merciful and True,
Father I thank You,
for who You are. Amen.

148. IT'S YOU

Written October 2001

I soar above the earth as on eagles wings,
cradled in Your loving arms,
abiding in You forever more.

It's You who brought me out of darkness.
It's You who cleansed and made me whole.
It's You who loved me even though . . . .
It's You who gave me hope and more.

Soaring up high in the sky,
fixed on eagles wings,
O' My God I love You so,
Ruler of everything in whom I adore.

It's You who brought me out of darkness.
It's You who cleansed and made me whole.
It's You who loved me even though . . . .
It's You who gave me hope and more.

I soar high above the earth,
as on eagles wings,
Your love and life has given me worth,
and set my heart to sing,
I love You forever more.

It's You who brought me out of the darkness.
It's You who cleansed and made me whole.
It's You who loved me even though . . . .
It's You who gave me hope for ever more.

It's You who brought me out of darkness.
It's You who cleansed and made me whole.
It's You who loved me even though . . . .
It's You who gave me hope forever more,
for ev—ver more. Amen.

149. I THANK YOU FATHER

Written October 2001

I thank you Father for my love;
Who is my Father up above.
I thank you Father for your Son;
Who took my place in death and won.
I thank you Father for the right;
To call you Father both day and night.
I thank you Father God Most High;
I need you Father and that's no lie. Amen.

150. EMPTY ME OUT

Written November 2001

Empty me out,
to fill me up.
Tare me down,
to build me up.
Fill me up,
to pour me out.

Teach me Your ways,
to walk day-by-day.
Keep me night and day,
to follow You come what may.
Help me know Your heart,
to love the whole not the part.

Rejoice and stand amazed,
to know His precious ways.
Call upon His name,
to find He is ever the same.
Pray Thy Kingdom Come,
to see God's will be done.

Empty me out,
to fill me up.
Tare me down,
to build me up.
Fill me up,
to pour me out.

Mold me like clay,
to fashion in Your way.
Lead me high and low,
to follow where You go.
Fill me with Your strength,
to finish running the race.

Choose which way you'll go,
to Heaven above or Hell below.
Caste your cares on Him,
to Jesus Christ The Saviour of all men.
Praise His Holy Name,
to lift Him high who took man's place.

Empty me out,
to fill me up.
Tare me down,
to build me up.
Fill me up,
to pour me out.

Work in me Your will,
to show that You are real.
Let me see Your light,
to follow even in the night.
Speak in me Your word,
to know it's You I've heard.

Take up your cross and follow Him,
to Kingdom living free from sin.
Look unto Him who shows us the way,
to rest in God everyday.
Put your trust in Him this day,
to keep you in His hand to stay.

Empty me out,
to fill me up.
Tear me down,
to build me up.
Fill me up,
to pour me out.
Amen.

151. HAPPY BIRTHDAY JESUS

Written December 2001

Happy Birthday Jesus,
Rejoice and praise His Holy name.
Happy Birthday Jesus,
He is forever the same.
Happy Birthday Jesus,
He loves us with a love so strong.
Happy Birthday Jesus,
He came to earth to make right all wrong.
Happy Birthday Jesus,
He lived and died and Lives again.
Happy Birthday Jesus,
He won the battle over Hell without Him for all men.
Happy Birthday Jesus,
in Him love, joy, and peace are so true.
Happy Birthday Jesus,
choose life in Him and be complete, too. Amen.

152. THIS FAMILY

Written December 2001

I was adopted into this family,
I am proud to call my own.
A sister to all my Father's children,
Young and old forever more.
I was adopted into this family,
whose head is love personified.
I was adopted into this family where love and life reside.
I was adopted into this family a king and priest on high.
Daughter of the Great I Am,
Almighty God Most High.
I was adopted into this family when my Father's Son became my Lord.
I was adopted into this family I'll praise and rejoice in Him for ever
more.
Jesus Christ is my Father's only begotten Son.
Elder Brother, King and Priest,
Lord and Saviour and a lot more.
Why you ask, how can this be?
Adopted by a Father you can not see.

Oh I can and yes I do,
in so many different ways.
He is in the light and beauty,
and heart filled love of all I can survey.
His touch is warm His arms are strong,
His love it knows no bounds.
He proved that when He gave His Son,
who died upon a tree shedding His blood for you and me.
For it was He who took our place,
and bore our sins who loves us all you see.
Open your heart and receive the love of the Father through His Son.
Be ye blessed and set free choosing The Father's love and life.
Harkin to the Father's call,
and what the Son has done for all.
Let Him adopt you into this family,
you are precious in His sight.
He calls you His beloved child,
and the apple of His eye,
so let Him adopt you into His family,
and walk with Him always by your side. Amen.

153. UNITED WE STAND, DIVIDED WE FALL

Written December 2001

United we stand,
divided we fall;
we need one another in the work to which we are called.
Hands holding hands,
we help one another when we lay our differences aside.
Each different from one another none being the same,
but all working towards that Glorious day.
The day when our Lord will come again,
and take us away to live with Him.
Until that day when we see His face,
there is a work needing to be done in this place.
So join the laborers in the field,
a goodly harvest has been revealed.
United we stand,
divided we fall,
lets show God's love to one and all. Amen.

154. LOVE

Written December 2001

Love is the key to open locked hearts.
Love binds up wounds of those we have not had a part.
Love opens the doors and welcomes us in.
Love looks not upon the color of your skin.
Love knows no bounds when God lives in men.
Love gives much more than it receives.
Love caused our Saviour to die on the tree,
taking the place of you and me.
Love picks us up whenever we fall.
Love comes running as soon as we call.
Love forgives sin and gives us a fresh start.
Love puts back together a broken heart.
Love is kindness as well as good.
Love says I knew you could not,
but I could.
Love builds up what hate tears down.
Love draws a smile out of a frown.
Love says let's use this not waste it on the shelf.
Love thinks of others above one's self.
The love of God is real and true,
won't you let Him love you, too. Amen.

155. SING A SONG TO OUR GOD MOST HIGH

Written January 2002

Sing a song of praise and thankfulness,
sing a song to He who gave us life.
Sing a song of praise and gratefulness,
sing a song to our God Most High.

Come and join in one our voices,
to the heavenly's up above the skies,
come and join in one our voices,
for Holy is our God Most High.

Sing a song of love and thankfulness,
sing a song to He who gave us life.
Sing a song of love and thankfulness,
to our God Most High. Amen.

156. COME DECLARE GOD'S GREATNESS

Written March 2002

Come and gather all ye children of the living God.
Lift your hands and your voices,
praising our God above.
Exalting His holy name,
acknowledging that You our God are forever the same.

Come and gather all ye children of the living God,
Lifting your eyes and your hearts,
rejoicing in God's love.
Exalting your holy name,
acknowledging that You our God are forever the same.

Come and gather all ye children of the living God,
Lifting your hands and your voices,
declaring the greatness of our God.
Exalting your name above all names,
and acknowledging that You our God are forever the same,
that You our God are forever the same. Amen.

157. I WILL DECLARE THY GREATNESS

Written April 2002

I will declare thy Greatness,
uttering the memory of thy great Goodness,
and shall sing of thy Righteousness to the end of the world.
The Lord is Gracious and full of Compassion,
slow to anger and filled with great Mercy.
The Lord is Good to all who come unto Him,
and His tender mercies are over all of His fold.
O' Lord hear thy children blessing thy Holy name.
They shall speak of the Glory of thy Kingdom and talk of thy power.
Let us exalt Your Holy name,
and acknowledge that You are God Almighty,
all Powerful, Holy, Righteous and True.
Call upon Jesus Christ,
God's only begotten Son,
and He will hear you never fear,
He will never leave nor forsake,
those who are truly His so do not faint.
God is Love,
God is True,
let Him be your Saviour, too. Amen.

158. YOU . . . .

Written May 2002

You make me strong when I was weak.
You make me whole when I was in lack.
You gave me hope when I had none.
You gave me life when I chose to follow Your Son.
You set my feet dry when I was sinking.
You set my heart right when I was turned wrong.
You gave me joy when I was empty.
You gave me love when I did not know how to love You back.
You make me glad when I could call You Father.
You make me cry for joy when You call me Your beloved. Amen.

159. FREE

Written April 2002

This gift that God gives is paid in full,
and there are no strings attached.
This gift that God has given could never have been paid in full by a
human being,
and that's a fact.
Jesus Christ the Lamb of God,
and God's only begotten Son,
winning the battle over death,
for in life He won.
Nothing to owe and nothing to pay,
except God's precious gift and be set free this day.
Accept this gift that was given to all man.
accept this gift sent by the Great I Am.
accept this gift free and clear.
for God is love and wants you to draw near. Amen.

160. IN NEWNESS OF LIFE

Written April 2002

I thank You Lord,
what else can I say.
My heart overflows with love for You each and every day.
My place upon the cross He bore,
My sins are for what His flesh was torn.
I Thank You Lord,
what more can I say,
my heart overflows with thankfulness and gratefulness each and every
day.

In newness of life I was restored by the Son.
In newness of life in Jesus I have won.
I thank You Lord,
what else can I say,
I love You Lord,
more and more each and every day. Amen.

161. ONE

Written April 2002

One you, one me, one hope,
and one tree.
One truth, one way, one road,
and one day.
One step, one light, one Lord,
and one life.
One you, one me,
and one God who set us free.
One Lord, one tree,
and one lamb of God who shed His blood for thee.
One step, one day,
and one light shed upon our way.
One truth, one Son,
and one hope in Jesus, for in Him we have won. Amen.

162. TELL-ME-TRULY

Written March 2001

There was a man born long, long ago,
and far, far away.
This very tall and simple man's name was Tell-Me-Truly.
Now this simple man, he walked the hills, valleys, fields, and woods
seemingly without care,
but Tell-Me-Truly was at home and had no fear there.
Then one day while on his way,
he ran into a child.
"Help me Sir", the child said.
"I'm lost, and all alone."
"Poor little child", said Tell-Me-Truly.
"Where is your home?"
"I Lie, is where I live, in that direction,
over some hills is my home", Said the child.
Now Tell-Me-Truly, truly was not afraid,
even though he had been told never to go that way.
He shook his head and shrugged his shoulders and said,
"It's too late to go today,
come along I'll take you home it's not that far,
you're welcome to stay."
"My name is Tell-Me-Truly,
what is your name my young lost lad."
The boy looked up and then looked down finally speaking these words,
"My name is Theodore, Jefferson, Rosey, Robert, Applesauce the Third,
but you can call me Bob for short."

"I want to go to my home,
I live in I Lie",
he pleaded all the way to Tell-Me-Truly's abode. His home was built tall
and wide,
and long sitting among the Silver Pines,
with flowers growing everywhere,
it looked so very fine.
"I'd like to take you to your home,
but I can't it's too late to start out today."
"Let's go in and eat some food and rest till day draws nigh",
said the big simple man with a heart full of compassion.
"Yes Sir, Mr. Tell-Me-Truly,
I'd best do what you say,
I found I am quite hungry,
and in need of rest for a new day".
In the morning it was raining so hard that the river topped its banks.
There was no traveling on that day nor two more besides.
By this time Bob was feeling very guilty for lying to this nice man.
"I wish I hadn't run away", Bob suddenly cried,
"I wish I hadn't run away,
getting lost was not for what I tried".
Tell-Me-Truly was not really very surprised to hear the words that
showed the lad had lied. "Is there something else you would like to
share",
Tell-Me-Truly calmly replied."
Well", Bob said with a down caste face,
"I Lie is not my home,
for I ran away from Jubilee Valley Children's Home,
that is where I stayed.
I was not happy there,
I want to have a real home,

I want someone to love me and feel that I belong".
"I see", said Tell-Me-Truly after some very deep thought.
"There is only one of me, but I'd be glad if you'd stay,
you see for I'd love a family in my home and a little boy to call my own".
Bob looked up with tears in his eyes and said,
"I am very sorry that I lied please forgive me", Bob cried,
"and if you really meant what you said,
I'd really love to stay and be your child".
Tell-Me-Truly smiled real big,
and opened wide his arms and said,
"I forgive you and I really want you to be my very own son and that's no
lie".
God's love is like that with His creations,
of which you are one.
When Jesus came down to earth,
He came to take our place.
Taking all upon Himself and nothing owing back is paid.

He came to die and rise again in fullness of life,
setting us free from sin.
God is love,
Jesus is life,
now we can receive mercy and grace in Christ.
Excepting Jesus as Lord and Saviour makes us children of our Father
God,
bringing close the family ties.
And God is looking down on us then with a great big smile,
and arms opened real wide as He welcomes us in and that's no lie.
Amen.

163. A LITTLE GIRL

Written May 2002

There was a little girl in town,
whose parents passed away.
Once she smiled,
but now she frowns all alone and afraid.
Won't somebody stop and help Sally find her way,
and give her what she really needs,
hope, love and a secure place.
Yes, a safe place to sleep,
good food to eat,
and nice clothes upon her back.
Give her what she really needs,
the love, the joy, and the peace.
Reach out to this little girl,
who does not know the way to go,
and point her to our Father God and watch her hurt heart go.
Turning what was meant for evil into something good.
And then we could say,
there was a little girl whose parents passed away,
but God He healed her broken heart and now she smiles all day. Amen.

Sherry Norton was born in 1957, the first of three children. At the time of her birth, her parents were living in Topeka, Kansas, assigned to Forbes Air Force Base. She grew up in various places, finally landing in Fayetteville, North Carolina, where she lived with her husband, Willie Clyde Norton, for thirty-three years before his death in 2010. She is a cancer survivor and has been visually impaired all her life. After being a member of a cult for twenty-three years, Sherry says only the love and intervention of her heavenly Father brought her out of deception and darkness and trying to live under the law with little love or hope.